The best thing about this carefully curated collection is that the poems gathered herein are anything but pious hymns and odes; rather, they address the concrete particularity of the everyday and the mystery of grace in a broken but beautiful creation. That's what makes them Catholic: the faith that inhabits these poems isn't sprinkled on top; it glows from within and illuminates the world around us.

—GREGORY WOLFE, Publisher, Slant Books, Author of *Beauty Will Save the World*

Bravo! This is a remarkable introduction not only to contemporary Catholic poetry, but to poetry in general. The poems are carefully chosen, consistently powerful, and truly catholic in their range. The introductions are engaging and useful. Rare is the book that's ideal as either a gift or a textbook. This one is.

—MIKE AQUILINA, Chairman of the Board, International Poetry Forum, and Author of *Rhymes' Reasons*

What an extraordinary collection of poets has been brought together here by April Lindner and Ryan Wilson in this profoundly moving panoply of twenty-three American voices covering the past seven decades, each in their way paying homage to the deep spiritual and existential concerns that haunt us all. Read it, friends, page by page by page, soak it all up and take in the music and pathos and beauty of what real poetry has to offer us.

—PAUL MARIANI, Author of *Deaths and Transfigurations, The Mystery of It All,* and *All That Will be New*

This is the definitive anthology of contemporary Catholic poetry in America and an important contribution to American letters more broadly. While deserving celebration among Catholic readers, the poets represented here merit much broader recognition. The wonderful poems in this anthology will delight, challenge, and move anyone interested in poetry.

—LEE OSER, Professor of English, College of the Holy Cross; Immediate Past President, Association of Literary Scholars, Critics, and Writers

Selective, startling, judiciously arranged—*Contemporary Catholic Poetry* is quite simply a gift to lovers of poetry, whatever their religious beliefs.

—MICAH MATTIX, Poetry Editor, *First Things*, Professor of English, Regent University, Co-editor, *Christian Poetry in America Since 1940*

This anthology should be a standard assignment in every Catholic school in the English-speaking world. From Julia Alvarez and Dana Gioia to James Matthew Wilson and David Yezzi, we have the most superb verse by poets eager to speak of human affairs through a Catholic lens that takes in the full range of despair, doubt, joy, love, uncertainty, death, and faith. "I conjure the perfect Easter," one of them writes; "I am the Angel with the Broken Wing," says another; and "Nightly angst, ennui, and gloom / Refine the human need for some perfection," says still another. These are thoughts given in eloquent words that young Catholics should ingest throughout their high school career. So, let's go, diocese superintendents: you now have a tool to make English a thoroughly Catholic experience. Use it.

—MARK BAUERLEIN, Senior Editor, *First Things*;
Author of *The Dumbest Generation Grows Up*

If the words "contemporary" and "Catholic" anywhere in proximity to the word "poetry" raise your eyebrows in alarm at fears of low artistic merit or dubious faith, April Lindner and Ryan Wilson's anthology *Contemporary Catholic Poetry* will challenge these assumptions in unexpected ways. With its wide array of prolific and award-winning poets and its expert preface tracing the development and flourishing of Catholic poetry in Europe and America, this collection will be one that teachers, editors, poets and poetry lovers alike can return to time and again to be fed by mastery of form, image and narrative and be strengthened with hope in an unbroken continuum for the Catholic Intellectual Tradition.

—MARY ANN B. MILLER, Founding Editor, *Presence: A Journal of Catholic Poetry*; Professor of English, Caldwell University

CONTEMPORARY CATHOLIC POETRY

AN ANTHOLOGY

EDITED BY

April Lindner and Ryan Wilson

IRON
PEN

PARACLETE PRESS
BREWSTER, MASSACHUSETTS

For Mike Aquilina, Brad Leithauser, and Ernest Suarez,
wonderful friends.
—Ryan Wilson

In memory of my grandmother,
Virginia Andros.
—April Lindner

2024 First Printing

Contemporary Catholic Poetry

Copyright © 2024 by Paraclete Press, Inc.

Hard cover: ISBN 978-1-64060-970-9
Paperback: ISBN 978-1-64060-646-3

The Iron Pen name and logo are trademarks of Paraclete Press.

Library of Congress Cataloging-in-Publication Data
Names: Lindner, April, editor. | Wilson, Ryan, 1982- editor.
Title: Contemporary Catholic poetry : an anthology / edited by April Lindner and Ryan Wilson.
Description: First printing. | Brewster, Massachusetts : Paraclete Press, 2024. | Summary: "A compilation
   of recent poetry that is appealing both to Catholic readers and to the general reading public"--
   Provided by publisher.
Identifiers: LCCN 2023058159 (print) | LCCN 2023058160 (ebook) | ISBN 9781640609709
   (hardcover) | ISBN 9781640606463 (paperback) | ISBN 9781640606487 (pdf) | ISBN
   9781640606470 (epub)
Subjects: LCSH: American poetry--Catholic authors. | BISAC: POETRY /
   Subjects & Themes / Inspirational & Religious | POETRY / American / General
Classification: LCC PS591.C3 C66 2024 (print) | LCC PS591.C3 (ebook) |
   DDC 811.6--dc23/eng/20240221
LC record available at https://lccn.loc.gov/2023058159
LC ebook record available at https://lccn.loc.gov/2023058160

10 9 8 7 6 5 4 3 2 1

Published by Paraclete Press
Brewster, Massachusetts
www.paracletepress.com

Printed in the United States of America

CONTENTS

WELCOME, ALL WONDERS: A PREFACE

Welcome, all wonders in one sight!
　　Eternity shut in a span,
Summer in winter, day in night,
　　Heaven in earth, and God in man.
Great little one! whose all-embracing birth
Lifts earth to Heav'n, stoops Heav'n to earth.

—Richard Crashaw

WHAT DO POEMS DO?

Amid the global pandemic and many upheavals of 2020, news broke about a team of archaeologists, led by a professor from Exeter University, who had discovered, deep in the Amazon rainforest of southern Colombia, an eight-mile-long wall of stone covered in artwork from more than 12,000 years ago. Among the tens of thousands of paintings are depictions of long-extinct Ice Age flora and fauna, such as the mastodon, and of masked human figures dancing, hand-in-hand, likely in some holy ritual forgotten eons ago. Many more of the paintings are simply images of a human being's hand: innumerable human hands from 10,000 years before the birth of Christ, from roughly 9,000 years before the siege of Troy represented in Homer's *Iliad*. Those humans who pressed their muddy hands against a stone wall so long ago are nameless now. Their entire civilization remains a mystery to us. And yet, their handprints, elaborate geometric designs, and exquisite paintings reveal to us glimmers from a lost world, each image speaking in a dazzling silence for its maker, illuminating our imaginations with the tacit assertion, "I was here."

In addition to its astonishing size, the wall has another remarkable feature: some of the paintings are at such a great elevation that they cannot even be viewed from the ground. How did anyone get up that high, that long ago? Why were these paintings made? Why climb to such perilous heights to leave a handprint? No doubt, archaeologists and art historians and all sorts of scholars will be studying this magnificent monument for centuries to come, and we shall be learning more and more about a vanished civilization.

Among innumerable other questions raised by such a miraculous archeological discovery is this one: why do humans take such pains to make art? Ultimately, such questions lead us deep down into that darkling realm where we must consider what it is to be a human being. For our present purposes, however, we might begin by delimiting the question: why do contemporary human beings make poems, and why should contemporary humans read poems? For more than two thousand years, questions of what poetry is, how it works and ought to work, why it's written, and why it should be read have nettled poets, readers, scholars, and critics. Before we address the role of poetry for people today, we should first consider yet another question: what do poems do?

Poems represent the world and the people who inhabit it: they introduce us to plants, animals, human characters, and highly specific places. They show us striking images that may be familiar to us or entirely eldritch, tell us about experiences that might be akin to our own or quite different from our own. They delight us, seduce us, inspire us, instruct us, mock us, condemn us, console us, and mourn us. They challenge us, protest against us, and, sometimes, they baffle us. They celebrate the glories of the created world and its people, and they commemorate momentous occasions; they also curse the cruelty and the horror of the world and its people, and they lament catastrophes. They imagine other people's lives and other worlds. They invoke deities and absences. They also speak intimately of heartfelt truths, describe local haunts, and address ordinary people directly. They meditate on living, on dying, and on the passage of time. They tell us stories, they tell us lies, and they tell us stories that reveal the truth through lying, to paraphrase the great painter Pablo Picasso. They enchant us with beauty and appall us with terror. Above all, poems remember. Each poem is, on a fundamental level, an act of remembrance, a kind of handprint pressed against the wall of Time.

With this in mind, we may shift to ancient Rome to consider our question about what poems do. The Romans of antiquity used a single word for the poet and for the prophet: *vates*. What do the poet and the prophet have in common? If we follow St. Thomas Aquinas in thinking of prophecy as that which reminds us of what we have known but have forgotten, perhaps the linking of the poet and the prophet will not seem so outrageous. Hundreds, if not thousands, of the world's best-loved poems belong to the *memento mori* tradition, the "remembrance of death" tradition. Why? This is so because we are always forgetting our own mortality. Drive down any interstate through any major city, and you're likely to encounter any number of drivers speeding, fiddling with phones, weaving in and out of lanes, and generally demonstrating that they are not particularly aware of their own mortality or of the mortality of others. Then again, many more of the world's best-loved poems belong to the *carpe diem* tradition, or "seize the day" tradition, dating back, at least, to the Roman poet Horace's Ode i.11, published in 23 BC, the source of that famous Latin tag. Why? Not only are we always forgetting our mortality, but we're also always being distracted from our purposes, drifting into procrastination, frittering our time away with unimportant concerns, watching silly YouTube videos, and so forth. Abstractly, we all know that we will perish and that we must make the most of our time on earth; however, in an immediate sense we are always forgetting this knowledge. We too frequently lack the spiritual discipline to keep these basic truths before the mind's eye. Consequently, a great many poems have reminded us, and continue to remind us, of these truths which we know but are always forgetting.

Because the human being is so forgetful, the memorization and recitation of poems have long been valued for their cultural functions. For instance, consider the oral Sumerian traditions passing along the *Gilgamesh* before it was written; consider the function of the Sutras, or of Homer's great catalogues; consider the rhapsodes we meet in Plato, or the Old Norse skalds and Anglo-Saxon scops passing along the *Beowulf*. Consider the vibrant and often violent world of the Tang dynasty as recorded by Tu Fu, or the extraordinary delicacies preserved in Bashō's haiku, or the rubicund and puckish realm of Chaucer's England. Times change, and the cultures of specific places change along with them, but poets seem always to be fending off forgetfulness. In all these poets, in fact, a version of meter, or measurement, has been retained to help us remember. Of course, what a given culture is in danger of forgetting shifts, and poets must shift accordingly, but poets are always reminding individuals of their era, and most especially reminding themselves, of those truths in danger of being forgotten, and poets are always attempting to give these reminders memorable form, enchanting form.

One of the things human beings are always forgetting is that the world is greater than any individual's idea of it. The world is more complex, more manifold, more mysterious than any mortal mind can fully comprehend, as is the human individual. And yet, in our desire for power and for comfort, we often forget this wildness, this elusiveness, this uncapturable quality. I am reminded, as readers familiar with the Buddhist tradition might be, of the "Diamond Sutra," in which the Buddha guides Subhuti toward a transcendence of his limited vision of reality. I'm also reminded of Euripides's great play *The Bacchae*, in which King Pentheus over and again tries to imprison the wild god Dionysus; of course, no prison can hold that fertility god from the East, and ultimately Pentheus is ripped limb from limb by the Bacchae (as a fertility god would traditionally be ripped limb from limb) in a paradoxical reversal, or *peripeteia*. In short, we deny the wildness of the world at our own peril. As Henry David Thoreau once wrote, "I've never met a man who was fully awake." Indeed, we drift into a kind of sleep, go about in a sort of somnolence, unaware of the cosmic drama unfolding around us and equally unaware of the spiritual drama stalking the boards and chewing the scenery within each of us. In this world of superabundant variety and bright vitality and fluorescing flux, we find ourselves, of all things, *bored*, for we forget the superabundant variety and vitality and flux and replace that reality in our minds with an illusory image of the world as a familiar and fully determined thing. We are, in fact, bored not with the world, but with our image of it, a reductive image which becomes commonplace.

What is too easily beheld is hardly seen. The fragile blossoms of our thoughts and words float upon a dark and fathomless river, yet we mistake the blossoms we can hold for the river we cannot. We become, in short, superstitious. The vocation of the poet, the calling of the poet, is perhaps first a call to awaken, a call to seek out that wildness, that strangeness of being which we can encounter only when we escape the prison of our own ready conceptions, when we slip through the bars of our customary habits of mind. And one of the most important reasons contemporary humans write poems is to make contact with that world outside the jailhouse of the rote routine, to reach out toward those wonders we have suspected, have sensed, maybe even have known, but cannot hold, cannot continually remember, those rare and miraculous moments of revelation.

So, having reflected on what poems do, we might now ask: why should any contemporary human read poems? The successful poem, like the successful magic trick, is a revelation more about the audience than about the artist. As the great theologian Jacques Maritain points out, all human beings possess the "poetic faculty"—the desire to make something beautiful—however, for various reasons, few human beings pursue the "poetic art." Ideally, poems articulate insights available to all human beings, guiding the audience toward new vistas, new vantage points from which we can discover truths new to us, see afresh old and familiar truths, and glimpse the promises of eternity from our foothold in the temporal.

In fact, the great Roman poet Horace, who was Poet Laureate during Rome's *aetas aurea*, or "golden age," tells us in his epistolary *Ars Poetica* that the aims of poetry are *aut prodesse...aut delectare*, "to delight or to instruct." As it happens, the best poems both delight and instruct us in some way. The successful poem must somehow interest us, charm us, draw us in, cast a spell on us before it can lead us toward any discovery. Poems want to give us language with which to express and understand ourselves.

If a poem can delight you in the way a painting you love delights you, if a poem can enchant you, it entices you to pay attention to it, and to yourself, in a way that we're unaccustomed to doing. It asks you to stop, to put aside your busy schedule and your daily routine, and to linger, to relish the delectable savor of it, and to think about why it's so delicious to you. "Wow," you might say, "I like this. But why do I like it so much?" In the case of a painting, your eyes may devour the lines or the colors, or a striking figure. In the case of a poem, you may roll lines around on your tongue like a dollop of honey, or you may, like Emily Dickinson, feel as if the top of your head had flown off in a moment of wild discovery. But only when you are enchanted, only when you are enraptured by the flavor of the work will you be inclined to pause, and to consider what has so enraptured you, and why—what is it in you that responds so powerfully to such a thing?

Far too often, contemporary Americans come to think they don't like poetry because they are erroneously led to believe that poetry is about ideas. It is not. There are ideas in poems, usually, and there are emotions, but of foremost importance is the relish of poems, the sudden, immediate "yes" that the right words can conjure. What's more, every good poem ever written was written, in a sense, for you: good poets don't write to be obscure, or difficult, or to run up footnotes like a score in some video game. No, good poets don't write to torture high school students and college students of the future. They write with the hope of bringing readers of their time, and of the future, delight, and perhaps a bit of instruction, too. Behind most good poems is a sound love of the world, of its things and peoples and places. Poems ask you, too, to pay attention to what was so loved as to be rendered lovingly for you, for all created things pass away. Imagine if some talented artisan made an exquisite crystal chandelier for you; that's something like a poem. It has its use: it can illuminate. However, a crystal chandelier is not one of those hideous fluorescent lights that are acquired cheaply; rather, it's a kind of illumination that is a gift, a beautiful gift whose function and beauty are inseparable. While all sorts of subtle patterns and meanings might be wrought into such a fancy chandelier, probably you'd rejoice just to have a beautiful light-source in your house. Just so, poets would like you to admire their craftsmanship, and to study their intricacies, but most of all they want to give you an illuminating gift. That gift is a token of remembrance.

THE DEVELOPMENT OF CATHOLIC POETRY
IN ENGLAND AND EUROPE

To place this collection in context, we should consider its poetic ancestry, as it were. The earliest English poem extant, "Cædmon's Hymn," composed miraculously by a cowherd working for the monastery at Whitby, comes down to us via the AD 731 book *Ecclesiastical History of the English People* by the Venerable Bede, a Catholic monk. Monasteries played important roles in other Old English masterpieces such as "The Dream of the Rood" and the *Beowulf.* Despite his lampooning corruption within the Church, the first great English-language poet whose name we know, Geoffrey Chaucer (c.1340s–1400), was Catholic, as was the visionary Margery Kempe (1373–1438?). The roots of English language poetry reach deep into the rich soil of the Faith.

The Catholic Church and England had a long, if at times uneasy, alliance. Under King Henry VIII and his Tudor successors, Catholics found England to be increasingly hostile. When King Henry VIII married Anne Boleyn in January of 1533, banishing his wife Catherine of Aragon to Kimbolton Castle, he set into motion his own provisional excommunication. As Caesar said, upon crossing the Rubicon, *Alea iacta est,* "The die is cast." In 1534, King Henry declared himself, via Parliament's passage of the Oath of Supremacy, the head of the new Church of England, institutionalizing a separation from Rome while also demanding that his subjects swear an oath of loyalty to his new church. Those who refused the oath faced imprisonment and execution. The fate of Catholicism in England and the fate of Catholic literature in the English language were altered forever, formed by the need to flourish in a hostile environment.

Under the reign of Henry's successors, religious divisions in England grew deeper still, a river of blood coursing through them. Elizabeth I went so far as to decree that being or harboring a Catholic priest in England was a crime punishable by death. Following years of torture, St. Robert Southwell, a Jesuit priest and author of the much-celebrated poem "The Burning Babe," suffered terribly for the crime of being a Catholic priest on English soil. In 1595 he was "drawn to Tyburn upon a hurdle, there to be hanged and cut down alive; his bowels to be burned before his face; his head to be stricken off; his body to be quartered and disposed at her majesty's pleasure."

Given the tyranny of the time, Catholicism in England withdrew into the shadows, Catholic writers being forced either to hide or renounce their faith. Raised a Catholic and taught by Jesuits, John Donne renounced Catholicism and published *Ignatius His Conclave* in 1611, a skewering satire against St. Ignatius Loyola and the Jesuits. Shakespeare, who was raised by Catholics and whose father had taken a vow of fidelity to the Catholic Church, seems to have kept private his adult religious loyalties, though saints appear frequently in his writing and the Catholic doctrine of Purgatory is of significance to his masterpiece *Hamlet*. Ben Jonson converted to Catholicism while imprisoned in 1598 and returned to the Church of England only when even more stringent anti-Catholic laws compelled him to do so in 1610. Alexander Pope, generally thought the greatest English-language poet of the eighteenth century, was a Catholic. But between Pope and the nineteenth-century Jesuit priest Gerard Manley Hopkins, no major Catholic poets are to be found in the English language. Certainly, the dearth of Catholic poets during this time may be attributed in large part to the tyrannical anti-Catholic laws in England, which caused many Catholics to flee England and resettle in more hospitable countries on the European continent.

──────── THE FLOURISHING OF EUROPEAN CATHOLIC POETRY ────────

Catholic poetry on the continent fared quite differently. During Elizabeth's reign in England, Spain experienced its literary Golden Age, highlighted by Catholic poets such as Fray Luis de León, St. Juan de la Cruz, Luis de Góngora, and Lope de Vega, the "Spanish Shakespeare" and inventor of the three-act tragedy. Around the same time, French poetry flourished with the literary movement *La Pléiade*, featuring Catholic poets such as Joachim du Bellay and Pierre de Ronsard. Catholic dramatists such as Molière and Racine dominated the seventeenth-century stage. In the nineteenth century, Catholic poets Charles Baudelaire, Paul Verlaine, and Arthur Rimbaud stood at the forefront of French letters.

It was not only these French writers who paved the way for Catholicism's return to prominence in English letters. In 1829 the Roman Catholic Relief Act repealed many of the oppressive anti-Catholic laws in England, making it much less unpleasant for Catholics to live there. The High Church Anglicanism of the Oxford Movement in the 1830s and 1840s sought to restore some Catholic traditions to the Church of England, and St. John Henry Newman's powerful and public conversion to Roman Catholicism in 1845 broke significant ground.

Meanwhile John Ruskin's influential writings and lectures at Oxford helped to bring about the Pre-Raphaelite Brotherhood, a group deeply influenced by Catholic Italian poets and artists of the Middle Ages, especially Dante Alighieri and his circle. In *The Renaissance* (1873), Walter Pater explored his devotion to beauty—especially the beauty of works by Catholic artists like Botticelli, Luca della Robbia, and Michelangelo. This devotion also opened a passageway for spiritual exploration, as chronicled in Pater's masterful novel, *Marius the Epicurean* (1885). In the novel, the protagonist Marius is drawn to the mysteries and rites of the early Catholic Church by their beauty. Combined with the relaxing of anti-Catholic laws, the cult of beauty blazed the trail by which writers of the Decadent generation would wend their way to Rome.

Across the Atlantic, Henry Wadsworth Longfellow also broke ground on behalf of Catholicism. From its inception, the United States harbored strong anti-Catholic biases that influenced the work of most major nineteenth-century writers. Despite such biases, Longfellow's cosmopolitanism and polyglotism led him to study deeply the languages and literatures of traditionally Catholic nations such as France, Spain, and Italy. His knowledge of other cultures also led him to believe that "Every human heart is human," as he wrote in his 1855 epic *The Song of Hiawatha*. As Professor of Modern Languages at Harvard, Longfellow went so far as to found The Dante Club, and even published the first American translation of Dante's *Divine Comedy*. He had written powerfully against slavery and against the United States' horrific and dehumanizing treatment of Native Americans: in translating Dante's masterpiece in the 1860s, he implicitly took a stand against America's long-standing anti-Catholic sentiments. What's more, Longfellow initiated a grand tradition of Dante scholars at Harvard, including Charles Eliot Norton, the Spanish philosopher George Santayana, and T. S. Eliot, whose lifelong devotion to Dante shaped Modern literature and opened the way for Catholic literature to thrive in mid-twentieth-century America.

As it happens, the so-called "Catholic Moment" in American literature would begin in London, England, where a young T. S. Eliot, abroad and working on his doctoral thesis in philosophy, would meet Ezra Pound. Both Pound and Eliot would go on to pursue projects deeply influenced by Dante, that greatest of all Catholic poets. Pound and Eliot promoted a vision of the literary work as a whole which is more than the sum of its parts. They believed that every part in a work must partake in a pattern that gives increased resonance to each constituent part. The resonating parts then give greater resonance to the whole. No line or passage has its meaning alone, no matter how beautiful. In a masterwork of literature, all parts, and all patterns, must work together, as they do in the towering cathedral of genius that is Dante's *Divine Comedy*.

─────── THE CATHOLIC MOMENT IN AMERICAN LITERATURE ───────

Oddly enough, this Dantesque conception of literature—adumbrated in ancient lyric poets like Sappho, Catullus, and Horace, and in the great epics—resides at the core of what contemporaries generally call "The New Criticism." This term is a kind of phantasm, conjured by a long-standing misreading of the preface to *Understanding Poetry* by Cleanth Brooks and Robert Penn Warren. Contrary to common belief, the so-called New Critics did not advocate ending literary study with the text itself; they advocated *beginning* literary study there. New Critics such as Eliot, John Crowe Ransom, and Ransom's students Brooks, Warren, and Allen Tate promoted a vision of the poem as a work whose parts should all partake in patterns and whose parts and patterns should all work in harmony. That is, the New Criticism was thoroughly Dantesque. Indeed, Allen Tate and his wife, the novelist Caroline Gordon, both converted to Catholicism. The generation of writers who grew up reading Brooks and Warren's textbooks not infrequently converted to Catholicism. And a number of cradle Catholics found this prevailing Dantesque aesthetic conducive to their own writing.

The result was the Catholic Moment in American literature. Between 1944 and 1969, Catholic writers received the Pulitzer Prize and the National Book Award for poetry and fiction nine times. Twice was a Catholic named Poet Laureate of the United States (then called the "Consultant to the Library of Congress"). A host of Catholic writers enjoyed renown in this period: Daniel and Ted Berrigan, John Berryman, Robert Fitzgerald, Isabella Gardner, Julien Green, Josephine Jacobsen, Jack Kerouac, Robert Lowell, Phyllis McGinley, Claude McKay, Thomas Merton, John Frederick Nims, Flannery O'Connor, Walker Percy, Katherine Anne Porter, J. F. Powers, Kenneth Rexroth, Allen Tate, Hisaye Yamamoto, and many more.

But for more than a half-century—since 1969—no practicing Catholic has served as US Poet Laureate. Only a handful of Catholic writers have won the Pulitzer Prize or the National Book Award. Many esteemed contemporary writers were raised as Catholics, are "cultural Catholics," or bear some influence from Catholicism; nonetheless, that brief Catholic Moment, during which the American public treated the theology of the Catholic Church respectfully, can seem like ancient history.

The Sacramental Vision of Contemporary American Catholic Poetry

Whether or not a Catholic Renaissance is forthcoming in America remains to be seen. Nevertheless, the variety of poets and poems in this anthology demonstrate that Catholic poetry is very much alive. In this volume, readers will find poems about figures drawn from ancient mythologies and figures drawn from Hollywood movies, poems about nature and poems about art, poems about violence and greed and hatred along with poems about mercy, humility, grace, and love, poems about the things of our contemporary lives and poems about the afterlife. Moreover, readers will encounter poems that deploy a variety of styles, schemata, and forms. There are outspoken poems and reticent poems, poems of minimalism and poems of extravagant figuration. There are narrative poems, Surrealist poems, historical poems, performative poems, and poems of prayer. There are prose poems and poems written in traditional forms such as the sonnet, the sestina, and *terza rima*, that form invented and given its most perfect iteration by Dante in his *Divine Comedy*.

Dante depicts Beatrice Portinari as a human embodiment of God's love, just as the God Who is Love assumed human embodiment through the kenosis of Christ. This realization of the divine within the mundane is, perhaps, the key to the entire Renaissance. Recalling that God, upon making the world, said it was good, and that He "so loved the world," as John 3:16 has it, "that He gave his only begotten Son" to it, Dante and the artists of the Renaissance strove to depict the eternal within the temporal, the universal within the local. The Platonic division between the *pleroma*—literally the "realm of fullness" but often rendered "the realm of forms"—and the *kenoma*, or the realm of "emptiness" where human beings live, was bridged when Christ entered into history. As a result, all things and creatures and human beings and human acts take part both in time and in eternity, in world history and in sacred history: reality itself, therefore, becomes sacramental, and all being becomes a wonder.

Amid the great variety of poems in this book, the reader will find a consistent commitment to this vision of reality as sacramental. Underlying these poems is an acute awareness that this world is a wonder, that each moment of every human being's life is a wonder. These poems ask us to slow down, to pay attention not only to the poems themselves but also to our own lives and the lives of others, to live more fully in the brief while that we are here, to make the most of each moment we're given—to welcome, in short, all wonders.

—Ryan Wilson

NOTES ON THE TEXT

The selections for each poet have not been organized chronologically. Rather, the editors have sought out aesthetically pleasing arrangements of selections that, in some cases, span decades and numerous volumes.

The date following each poem is the date of the poem's first publication within a full-length collection.

Several of the poems include epigraphs, dedications, and the like. In some cases, formatting for these materials has varied from poem to poem throughout a poet's career, or even within a single book. For each such poem, the editors have followed the formatting of the text as it appeared in the most recent book publication of the poem.

Similarly, some poets begin each new line with a capital letter; others use capital letters only for proper nouns or for the initial word of a new sentence. Some poets alternate between these methods. In every case, the editors have followed the capitalization of the poem as it appeared in its most recent book publication.

In a very few instances, the editors have emended typographical errors that appeared in poems' original book publications.

Occasionally, the editors have included footnotes. If a footnote is drawn from the author of a poem, the author's note is credited.

EDITORIAL NOTES

In putting together an anthology of Contemporary Catholic Poetry, an editor must first determine what is meant by each of the constituent terms. How does one define what is contemporary and what isn't? Similarly, how does one determine if a writer is a Catholic writer or not? Finally, how does one define poetry? These questions are more complex than they may, at first glance, appear to be.

In determining what constitutes Contemporary Catholic Poetry, we should perhaps begin with the first term: *Contemporary*. The editors of this anthology have included only writers born in 1950 or afterward. Why should 1950 be the dividing line? First, several leading figures in contemporary Catholic poetry were born in 1950: Julia Alvarez, Maryann Corbett, Carolyn Forché, Dana Gioia, and Marie Howe. We agreed immediately to include these poets, and their common birth year of 1950 provided a logical boundary. Nonetheless, setting the dividing line at 1950 required the exclusion of several wonderful poets, some of whom happen to be acquaintances or friends of the editors. For instance, the editors very much admire the poems of William Baer (1948), but he is excluded. If we were to include Mr. Baer, why not also include the marvelous poet Paul Mariani (1940)? And if we were to include Mariani, why not the equally marvelous Samuel Hazo (1928)? Of course, if we were to include Prof. Hazo, who was publishing books in the 1950s, why not John Berryman (1914–1972), Robert Lowell (1917–1977), Phyllis McGinley (1905–1978), or Allen Tate (1899–1979), all of whom were also publishing in the 1950s? Without distinct boundaries the anthology's contents might have expanded exponentially, resulting in many fine writers of our time having their selections greatly diminished or excluded. While Baer, Mariani, and Hazo all continue to publish terrific books, which the editors encourage readers to seek out, the most practical, if lamentably imperfect, decision was to set the dividing line at 1950.

In considering the Catholicism of the poets included, the editors have assumed a similarly practical position. By the Church's own doctrine, anyone baptized into the Roman Catholic Church is a Catholic; however, a great many writers who were so baptized have openly repudiated the Church and do not recognize themselves as Catholics. Respecting their own assertions of religious identity, the editors have not included such writers. Rather, we have included only writers who have not publicly and categorically disavowed Catholicism, who are writing from within the context of their faith. The editors have not, of course, in any way attempted a kind of Inquisition: we have not, for instance, checked attendance records at Mass. Nor have we made specific Catholic content a criterion for a poem's inclusion, although we were pleased to note the myriad ways the Church has left its mark on the imaginations of these notable contemporary poets.

One question remains: how does one define poetry? While the definitions of poetry are seemingly innumerable, many of them worthy of long contemplation, we felt it would be imprudent to make this anthology in the image of any particular aesthetic manifesto. We have featured prose poems, free verse poems, and poems adhering to inherited forms. We have featured outspoken political poems and quietly personal poems, performative poems and meditative poems. In short, we have featured those poems we consider the strongest by the selected writers. To that effect, we have not shied away from choosing longer poems, which are so often omitted from anthologies.

Contemporary Catholic Poetry is not monolithic. The poets in this anthology do not share an aesthetic style, a political vision, a socio-economic background, a racial background, or a geographical background: "In my Father's house there are many dwelling places" (John 14:2). Indeed, the editors' ambition has been to bring attention to and to extol the variety of contemporary Catholic poems and poets, confident that wonderful treasures may be found in all the dwelling places of our Father's house.

Inevitably, some readers may quibble with the exclusion of a certain poet or the inclusion of certain poems; for whatever faults may be found in this anthology, the editors assume responsibility. We have done our best, in putting together this anthology (from the Greek *anthos*, or "flower"), to assemble a bouquet pleasing both to Catholic readers and to the general reading public. In short, we give this book in the spirit of a gift, and we hope it will be a welcome one.

R.W.
A.L.

CONTEMPORARY CATHOLIC POETRY

Julia Alvarez (1950)

Born in New York City, the second of four daughters, Julia Alvarez spent the first decade of her life in the Dominican Republic. When her father took part in an underground cell to overthrow dictator Rafael Trujillo, the cell was "cracked" by the secret police, and those not captured fled. The family was forced to return to the United States, where they settled in Queens, New York. The only Latin American students in her Catholic school, Alvarez and her sisters faced prejudice and alienation. She turned to literature for solace. At thirteen she was sent to boarding school, but spent summers with her family in the Dominican Republic.

Alvarez went on to study at Connecticut College, Middlebury College, and Syracuse University. After earning her master's degree, she served as a writer-in-residence for the Kentucky Arts Commission, conducting writing workshops and giving readings at elementary schools, high schools, and colleges throughout Kentucky. Alvarez has since taught at the University of Vermont, the University of Illinois, Middlebury College, and other schools. She resides in the Champlain Valley in Vermont with her husband, Bill Eichner, an ophthalmologist. Together they created Alta Gracia, a farm that promotes literacy and education, and later donated it to the Mariposa DR Foundation.

Alvarez's crystalline, accessible poems explore her identity as a Dominican American and the societal expectations of women in both cultures. Widely considered among the most prominent Latina writers, Alvarez has received the Pura Belpré and Américas Awards, the Hispanic Heritage Award, and the F. Scott Fitzgerald Award. In 2013 she was awarded the National Medal of Arts by President Barack Obama. The citation for that award praises Alvarez for her "extraordinary storytelling" and for how her work "illustrates the complexity of navigating two worlds and reveals the human capacity for strength in the face of oppression." In addition to poetry, Alvarez writes novels, nonfiction, and books for young readers.

Selected Bibliography
Poems: *The Other Side/El Otro Lado* (1995); *Homecoming: New and Collected Poems* (1996); *The Woman I Kept to Myself* (2011). Novels: *How the García Girls Lost Their Accents* (1991); *In the Time of Butterflies* (1994); *Afterlife* (2020). Nonfiction: *Once Upon a Quinceañera* (2008).

How I Learned to Sweep

My mother never taught me sweeping.
One afternoon she found me watching
t.v. She eyed the dusty floor
boldly, and put a broom before
me and said she'd like to be able
to eat her dinner off that table,
and nodded at my feet, then left.
I knew right off what she expected
and went at it. I stepped and swept;
the t.v. blared the news; I kept
my mind on what I had to do,
until in minutes, I was through.
Her floor was as immaculate
as a just-washed dinner plate.
I waited for her to return
and turned to watch the President,
live from the White House, talk of war:
in the Far East our soldiers were
landing in their helicopters
into jungles their propellers
swept like weeds seen underwater
while perplexing shots were fired
from those beautiful green gardens
into which these dragonflies
filled with little men descended.
I got up and swept again
as they fell out of the sky.
I swept all the harder when
I watched a dozen of them die.
as if their dust fell through the screen
upon the floor I had just cleaned.
She came back and turned the dial;
the screen went dark. *That's beautiful,*
she said, and ran her clean hand through
my hair, and on, over the window-
sill, coffee table, rocker, desk,

and held it up—I held my breath—
That's beautiful, she said, impressed,
she hadn't found a speck of death.

1984

FOLDING MY CLOTHES

Tenderly she would take them down and fold
the arms in and fold again where my back
should go until she made a small
tight square of my chest, a knot of socks
where my feet blossomed into toes,
a stack of denim from the waist down,
my panties strictly packed into the size
of handkerchiefs on which no trace
of tears showed. All of me under control.

But there was tenderness, the careful matching
of arm to arm, the smoothing of wrinkles,
every button buttoned on the checkered blouse
I disobeyed in. There was sweet order
in those scented drawers, party dresses
perfect as pictures in the back of the closet—
until I put them on, breathing life back
into those abstract shapes of who I was
which she found so much easier to love.

1984

SPIC
U.S.A., 1960

Out in the playground, kids were shouting *Spic!*
Lifting my sister's skirt, yanking her slip.
Younger, less sexy, I was held and stripped
of coat and bookbag. Homework tumbled out
into oncoming traffic on the street.
Irregular verbs crumpled under tires
of frantic taxis, blew against the grates
of uptown buses we would later take
when school let out, trailed by cries of *Spic!*
What did they want, these American kids?

That night when we asked Mami, she explained:
our classmates had been asking us to *speak,*
not to be so unfriendly, running off
without a word. "This is América!
The anthem here invites its citizens
to speak up. *Oh see, can you say,*" she sang,
proving her point, making us sing along.
She winked at Papi, who had not joined in
but bowed his head, speaking instead to God
to protect his daughters in America.

I took her at her word: I raised my hand,
speaking up during classes, recess time.
The boys got meaner. *Spic ball!* they called out,
tossing off my school beanie, playing catch
while I ran boy to boy to get it back.
They sacked my stolen lunch box for their snacks,
dumping the foreign things in the garbage bin,
Spic trash! But I kept talking, telling them
how someday when I'd learn their language well,
I'd say what I'd seen in America.

2004

Bilingual Sestina

Some things I have to say aren't getting said
in this snowy, blond, blue-eyed, gum-chewing English:
dawn's early light sifting through *persianas* closed
the night before by dark-skinned girls whose words
evoke *cama, aposento, sueños* in *nombres*
from that first world I can't translate from Spanish.

Gladys, Rosario, Altagracia—the sounds of Spanish
wash over me like warm island waters as I say
your soothing names: a child again learning the *nombres*
of things you point to in the world before English
turned *sol, tierra, cielo, luna* to vocabulary words—
sun, earth, sky, moon. Language closed

like the touch sensitive *morivivi* whose leaves closed
when we kids poked them, astonished. Even Spanish
failed us back then when we saw how frail a word is
when faced with the thing it names. How saying
its name won't always summon up in Spanish or English
the full blown genie from the bottled *nombre*.

Gladys, I summon you back by saying your *nombre*.
Open up again the house of slatted windows closed
since childhood, where *palabras* left behind for English
stand dusty and awkward in neglected Spanish.
Rosario, muse of *el patio*, sing in me and through me say
that world again, begin first with those first words

you put in my mouth as you pointed to the world—
not Adam, not God, but a country girl numbering
the stars, the blades of grass, warming the sun by saying,
¡Qué calor! as you opened up the morning closed
inside the night until you sang in Spanish,
Estas son las mañanitas, and listening in bed, no English

yet in my head to confuse me with translations, no English
doubling the world with synonyms, no dizzying array of words
—the world was simple and intact in Spanish—
luna, sol, casa, luz, flor, as if the *nombres*
were the outer skin of things, as if words were so close
one left a mist of breath on things by saying

their names, an intimacy I now yearn for in English—
words so close to what I mean that I almost hear my Spanish
heart beating, beating inside what I say *en inglés.*

1995

Ned Balbo (1959)

Ned Balbo was born in 1959 on Long Island, New York. While separated from the father of her first son, Balbo's birth mother began a relationship with Balbo's father, which resulted in two more children—Balbo and his older sister—who were raised in separate households by other family members. Both children grew up believing that their guardians were their parents, a pretense considered necessary to ensure that Balbo's birth mother would not lose custody of her first son during contentious divorce proceedings. Although Balbo's birth parents did eventually marry, the risk to custody—and belief in the need to maintain these arrangements—remained. Many of Balbo's poems explore aspects of this experience, touching on questions of identity, impostership, kinship, and connection. Against the gravity of these themes the poet often counterpoints wordplay, formal ingenuity, popular culture references, and comic irony.

Balbo received his bachelor's degree from Vassar College, and he holds graduate degrees from The Writing Seminars at The Johns Hopkins University and from The Iowa Writers' Workshop. His work has been awarded many prizes and honors, including The Towson University Prize for Literature, The Ernest Sandeen Prize in Poetry, The ForeWord Magazine Book of the Year, The Donald Justice Poetry Prize, The Richard Wilbur Prize, The New Criterion Prize, The Poets' Prize, and grants from the Maryland State Arts Council and from the NEA.

Remarkable for their sensitivity, especially toward those who are made to feel themselves outcasts, Balbo's poems, like Elizabeth Bishop's, tend to focus on subjects often overlooked, for one reason or another, in poetry. As Erica Dawson has noted, "Ned Balbo's eye for detail is so keen, you'll find yourself squinting at the page, hoping to find even more. And you do." Whether turning his attention to his personal life, the life of working-class suburbs in Long Island, nature, or old monster movies, Balbo is, as David Yezzi has said, a "wizard of the workaday."

Selected Bibliography
Galileo's Banquet (1998); *Lives of the Sleepers* (2005); *The Trials of Edgar Poe and Other Poems* (2010); *Upcycling Paumanok* (2016); *3 Nights of the Perseids* (2019); *The Cylburn Touch-Me-Nots* (2019).

SON OF FRANKENSTEIN

After James Whale's *Frankenstein*, 1931

Whose son am I? I woke alone, in thunder,
shocked from sleep, face bandaged, lightning flashing
through the gauze, the noise of chains and pulleys
guiding my descent from storm and chaos
back to consciousness, my father's voice—
I thought he was my father—crying out
in triumph, *It's alive!* I was an *it*,
newborn, created *thing*, though I could think,
almost, too weak to move, my frail hand,
stitched at the wrist, groping as if to touch
some other who might steady me, but, failing,
fallen at my side. I had a name—
what was it? Lost for good in convolutions
of a brain—imperfect, criminal—

both mind and not mine. Who was I then?
Nothing made sense: twice born, expendable,
I stared out from a stranger's face, my true voice
garbled by an injured lobe's short circuit.
And so, the weeks passed: locked within a cell
grave-deep beneath the watchtower where my father's
labor took its course, I never slept,
he seldom did: dank stone, a hunchback's torch
and torture—all the blind rage of a brother
suddenly displaced—brought down the whip
that punished flesh recoiling from fire.
I wanted light—not so much it would burn—
to know, but not so much that I'd shrink back,
repulsed by what I heard; to learn the reason

I was born, or made, or spat from darkness.
Now that I know the truth—which theft was botched,
what dream destroyed, my own dumb grunts the proof
I'm not who I should have been—my father

talks on, still so sure I'll never grasp
what crackles in electrodes, or in clouds.
What would I say if I could form the words?
Father, you're wrong. I, too, descend from Adam,
and this flesh I wear belongs to all
who came before, not just to you alone.
I'm yours—my father's son, and no one's son,
a blank face written off, some unnamed orphan
you'd discard if it would serve your purpose,
and the son you cannot welcome home.

2001

Miraculous Spirals

Spira Mirabilis, the logarithmic or "miraculous" spiral that widens
with every curve yet maintains its shape, is observed in astronomy,
biology, meteorology, coastal erosion, etc.

Upon a beach & under galaxies
            revolving, filled with stars,
     coiled on itself, a nautilus
      whose spiral is "miraculous"
lies tiger-striped, sea-scoured, its sacristies

more proof of nature's winding symmetries.
            A wave confronts the shore's
     unraveling resolve, the loss
      of coastal sand disastrous,
the crescent of its carving, by degrees,

a slow retreat…Unleashed, a storm gives rise
            to more than just brute force
     shaped like a wheel, calamitous:

its track is heading straight for us,
winds gaining speed… Far off, a raptor's eyes
catch sight of prey, pursuit we recognize
                    by how it dives, its course

        a gyre determined, dangerous
        (& logarithmic, more or less)
till—sated, safe—it shelters in the trees,
beneath the limbs a hurricane will seize.

An insect whirls, dizzy as it flies
                    in search of any source
            that shines, however hazardous.
            Translucent wings, diaphanous,
dry up in heat: stuck to the lamp, it dies,

fooled by synthetic sun. More mysteries:
                    the eye's corneal layers
            (a shield for its glassy surface,
            tender, tear-fed, aqueous)
resolve into a helix, vortices

of bundled nerves . . . What joins us all to these?
                    Time's pulse; the spirals' laws
            or hidden presence, marvelous

        & all-pervasive, measureless.
The nautilus, left on the sand to freeze,
holds thirty chambers, small eternities
                    that no one occupies,

        yet time & space are limitless
        & time itself may have to pass
before we learn the same geometries
reside in our unfolding destinies.

                    2019

Hart Island[1]

Only God knows the full history of this island...

I.

Only by ferry can you travel there—
Long Island Sound beneath, a few gulls whirling,
as you leave from City Island's coast
south of Pelham Bay, Manhattan's skyline
to the west, gray-blue, diminishing.
Behind you: trickle of whitecaps, chain of kelp,
the ferry landing's flag at Fordham Street—
From one world to the next you make your crossing
toward a shore not half a mile away.
Hart Island: heart-shaped only from the ocean
gray beneath the sign that warns, *Keep Off.*
Waves of rushes pulse below the hillside,
dead tree sheared in half, deserted beach.

At night, teenagers glide past, douse the lights,
and cut the engine, curious, or speed off,
avoiding Coast Guard boats that roam the waters
on patrol. By day, no one may visit
without an application, clearance, escort
by New York's Department of Corrections
which maintains the outpost: history's
last checkpoint for the lost or disappeared.

Who works here? Convicts, guards joined to one purpose:
bury the dead, the unidentified,
the destitute unclaimed in city morgues,
the lost, the homeless no one wants to see.
The cost is light—obedience and labor—
though the knowledge that they gain is hard:

---

1   "'Hart Island' takes its inspiration from Melinda Hunt and Joel Sternfeld's extraordinary book
of text and photographs, *Hart Island* (Zürich: Scalo Publishers, 1992). The epigraph quotes Albert
Carrasquillo (Pito), an inmate interviewed by the authors; italicized lines within the poem para-
phrase the remarks of other prisoners on Hart Island burial detail." [Balbo's note]

what lies ahead for those without a family,
those in exile, those who die alone.

The air is clear, sea-air; high grass brushed back
by salt wind. Squads of first offenders gather
(slaves' descendants, sons of immigrants)
under the eyes of officers in blue
for burials, groundskeeping, disinterments
that give order to their days, or years.

II.

What do the island's hundred acres hold?
The past's debris, jettisoned artifacts,
wrecked buildings, junk; the living and the dead;
ruins and new graves; dirt roads, fields of grass,
fresh ground kept waiting, woodlands overgrown.

Among those held against their will were soldiers,
Confederate infantry, their makeshift jail
the wooden barracks Union troops had used
during their training on Hart Island's hills.
The camp swelled to three thousand at its worst,
"graybacks" mixed with vagrants, local thugs
thrown under arrest, thirsty, shaking with fever—
Over two hundred in three months would die.
A wall of river-stones still marks the hillside
where both armies' dead once lay together
killed by disease or bullets, though their bodies,
during the Great Depression, were exhumed.
The Union soldiers' headstones showed their names;
their adversaries were anonymous.
Now all lie elsewhere, dead with equal honor,
whatever the cause they fought for, or against.

Before that, it was Indian land, of course,
the Siwanoys' ancestral home, the treaty

that renounced it swindling those who signed—
"savages" with no status under law.
Where did they go? They left—no trace remains—
but weren't the only tribe driven away
by force or fraud. Requesting sanctuary
in New Amsterdam from brutal Mohawks,
the Wappingers, too trusting, found betrayal:
the same Dutch governor who'd promised shelter
through interpreters honored his guests
by ordering their deaths. A thousand fell,
a tenth of their number, to his soldiers' guns.

Deception, blood, and brute force won the land.
One tribe less meant less trouble to the Crown,
the governor and his men had strategized.

Hart Island, too, fell under his command.

III.

Geese break from the marshland, fill the sky
with bleats and beating wings, brick carriage house
and bleak reformatory in the crescent
of an unnamed cove. Here, orphaned boys
once learned a trade beyond those that had brought
survival in the streets then brought them here
without recourse, a butcher's knives and hatchets
put to good use, this time, in their hands.
Others bent over benches scored with cuts
and curse-words, locked in, nailing soles to leather;
still more wielded tongs to twist hot iron
lit from within, burnt-orange, shedding sparks;
some inhaled the salt air, chopped the earth,
dropped seeds in furrows, plowed, or mortared walls—
those thousand chores that, mastered, ran the island,
saved boys from themselves, and set them free.

Those boys are men long dead, the buildings shells.

A rusted butcher's scale hangs untouched
beside a wall case emptied of its knives.
The silhouettes of hand-saws used for meat
(long lost or looted) mark the workhouse walls.

IV.

By 1887, Jacob Riis—
reporter and amateur photographer
appalled by slum conditions—found the means
to bring the truth to light. The means *was* light,
magnesium's spark and flash, the *Blitzlichtpulver*
that exploded darkness from the walls
of windowless tenements whose panicked tenants
fled the room for fear of being burned.
The cause was worth it. Soon the world would see,
captured on glass plates, grief and poverty
few knew beyond the multitudes who lived
its daily deprivations. People *paid*
to hear Riis lecture while his "magic lantern,"
one view fading while the next appeared,
projected on church walls or linen screens
the lives of those he'd now illuminate:
mothers in bare rooms, seated next to barrels,
bellows or buckets, babies in their arms;
"street arabs" (orphaned boys) locked arm in arm,
asleep, or drunk, in alleys, who dared declare,
awake, to Riis, "We didn't live nowhere."

The public ate it up, and Riis was made.
New Yorker, Danish immigrant, reformer,
he kept up his photographic "raids"
on those he called "the Other Half." And, once,
unnerved by a "thousand, helpless human wrecks"
smoking clay pipes and hurling abuse

at those who passed, angry at all they'd lost
or thrown away, afraid of what was next,
Riis asked the Blackwell Island's workhouse warden
if he might "take" them, meaning "take their picture,"
but received these words as his response:
Take them? Yes, take all thousand, if you like—
you're welcome to 'em. They'll never quiet down
until they reach Hart Island in a box—
No doubt they'll gripe about their funeral.

V.

Barbed wire tops the fence, guards watch the shore
today where prisoners, half-entrenched, receive
those that the earth will keep, as men have done
here for some portion of three centuries.
When space was needed, New York found it here:
a madhouse, workhouse, women's hospital,
and more, had roots here, once, before they failed,
contributing their share among the dead.

Once, Riis recalled, struck by the shuffling host
of women taking their therapeutic walk
in dresses asylum-gray, dead-eyed or manic,
he heard, from a barred cell near, one woman singing,
Oh, how my heart grows weary, while the ranks
of "lunatics," as he called them, stirred or screamed,
rankled, elated by sound. On this tour
of the Blackwell's women's sanitarium
whose overflow Hart Island housed and held,
"A hopeless case," her doctor murmured, turning,
escorting Riis politely on his way.

Hart Island's men, who clear the pits, are sane.
The ferry they await will bring the morgue
truck which, in turn, will make its way to them
along paved roads or mud trails, sun or rain.

The convicts know its cargo is themselves,
or might as well be; none is in a rush,
most of the time, to start the job or finish.
What is the final plot or destination
of the plywood coffins that they bear,
or of the stranger that each box contains?

Names aren't needed. Sharing each long trench,
boxed bodies lie arranged in rows, mass graves
soon to be filled, the "unbefriended dead"—
all those who die unclaimed—erased at last.

I used to joke, Just throw me in the ditch,
I won't mind when I'm dead. Now I'm not sure.
Maybe I'll write a will when I get out
so I don't end up in a place like this.

A few on burial detail nod their heads.

VI.

Their forebears, in a world war's aftermath,
tired of digging graves, the world a grave,
sought out a labor to affirm their faith,
gaze lifted from the gravesite to the sky.
Petition heard, they built a monument
visible from the sea, its whitewashed concrete
rising over grassland, open fields,
woods, the warden's house; carved on its surface
PEACE: that one word. Cry of gratitude,
prayer's object during war, its own reply.

Here, too, a Cold War missile base lies rusting
underground, abandoned like the ballfield
where a jailhouse team once played the soldiers
who maintained our national defense.
Convicts battled conscripts, ran the diamond,

free within its boundaries, slamming hits
or throwing strikeouts that the New York press,
invited guests, could celebrate in print,
cooperating with officers and guards
who filled up bleachers shipped from Ebbets Field.

(Yes, the Dodgers' park: a demolition
Brooklyn's cries of outrage couldn't stop,
a loss mourned longer than most buried here,
longer than most who do the burying.)

Sometimes I wish they'd let us out at night
when everything is still so I could see
what happens, get the feel of what it's like....
I don't fear death and do what I am told.

VII.

Of children—infants, immigrant or native—
nineteenth-century clerks, in cursive hand,
preserved the full name, birthplace, cause of death,
until too many lives, too many deaths
broke down the custom. Later burial books
yield last names only, as if children died
in numbers past all hope of keeping records
up to date, wound, injury or illness
labelled "confidential" or left blank.
The grave of one child, though, is an exception:
far from the "baby trenches," common graves
that hold a thousand children, set apart
in deep woods, hidden by grass, the concrete marker
SC-B1 1985
warns off those who approach New York's first child
to die of AIDS, the mother who'd have mourned
already dead. A body set aside
in fear, forgotten: no one's son or daughter.

VIII.

"My grandparents lived there in a big white house—
Hart Island was their home. I see it now,
sun on the sun porch windows, rows of maples
shading the sidewalks where I played with friends,
rode bikes or roller-skated. Staff lived there
—my Grandpop was the Welfare Superintendent—
and it was like its own town, its own world,
the sea-wind and the sound of the sea at night—
nothing scary about it. When I stayed over
I saw the shelter and, sometimes, the men,
who seemed all right: healthy and hard at work.
And I remember, while Grandmom clasped my hands,
repeating her words of blessing for those men—

Hart Island was where I first learned how to pray."

IX.

To Riis, a doctor friend confided once
what both already knew, as if the telling
would relieve the grief: "Many a mother,
her child about to die, has wept in panic,
'Doctor, I can't afford to bury it,'
as if my knowing this would change the outcome
God and my limitations preordained;
and when the child's breathing stops, she'll cry
as much for where she'll find the burial money
as for the death itself. So human sorrow
dies, too, in the slums." And so Hart Island,
Riis knew, waits for losses such as these.

His slide show, dazzling to the audience
who viewed the lecture both to ease their conscience
and glimpse lives they thanked God weren't their own,
closed with the full array of last addresses
possible for the poor: the New York Morgue,

the Blackwell's Island Penitentiary,
the Lunatic Asylum on Ward's Island,
Bellevue, and, his parting shot, Hart Island,
the first that Riis had taken on his own,
wearing his greatcoat, January snows
frozen along the dirt trails and the beach
from which he trudged, weighed down by his equipment,
one or two assistants at his bootheels,
under a blank white sky.
                     He caught the view:
an open grave. The shot was overexposed
but served its purpose when the image lingered
on the wall before the magic lantern
shut down to the hiss of hydrogen
and burning lime, and everyone went home.

X.

The ferry's close, the crossing's almost over.
I haven't been here long but always thought
that everyone would come to pay respects—
family, friends—but we just watch the tractors
dig the hole, and throw the coffins in.
Here, where griefs are carried, graves exhumed
each quarter century, the same earth used,
dug up again, bone fragments lie exposed
where beach erodes. Stop now:
                     the new arrivals,
living and dead, so many long forgotten
occupy the same ground: potter's field,
the first of which, Saint Matthew tells—blood-purchased,
set aside by law—held strangers, too.
You are among them now. Manhattan's icons
glitter under haze. Canada geese,
black-necked and white-cheeked, nest, or root, or wander
on the beach, or take off from the rocks
in flight from shore to shore.

The nameless dead,
the numbered penitent await you here,
their term like yours uncertain, short years served
upon an island you must not call home.

2010

Molly McCully Brown (1991)

Molly McCully Brown grew up on the campus of Sweet Briar College, Virginia, where her parents taught English. Inspired to write at an early age, Brown has stated in an interview in *The Adroit Journal*, "As soon as I could hold a pen, that was it for me. I've never really wanted to do anything else." Brown earned an associate's degree from Bard College, a BA from Stanford University, and an MFA in creative writing and poetry from the University of Mississippi.

Complications at birth left Brown with cerebral palsy, in need of numerous surgeries and a wheelchair. Her identical twin sister, Frances, died within thirty-six hours of their births. One summer in her college years, Brown and a friend stopped to explore the grounds of the former Virginia State Colony for Epileptics and Feebleminded, a state-run residential hospital which isolated people with mental and physical disabilities from the rest of society. Brown had grown up a short drive from the facility, but seeing its buildings and cemetery up close led to a stark epiphany: if she'd been born fifty years sooner, she might have been sent to live there herself. Brown says the thought "was moving and complicated and hard. I'm attached to that part of the world. I know and love the landscape. These were my roots." That realization informed her first poetry collection, *The Virginia State Colony for Epileptics and Feebleminded*. Set in the 1930s, the volume interweaves poems in the voices of imagined patients and staff. *The New York Times* called the book "part history lesson, part séance, part ode to dread." With Susannah Nevison, Brown also co-authored an epistolary poetry collection, *In the Field Between Us*.

Brown has written essays about her experience as a recipient of the prestigious Amy Lowell Scholarship, which enabled her to live in Bologna, London, and Cardiff and to travel to Madrid, Dublin, and Paris. She has also written about her conversion to Catholicism, her mistrust of religious fundamentalism, and the death of her twin. A recipient of a United States Artists Fellowship, a Civitella Ranieri Foundation Fellowship, and the Jeff Baskin Writers Fellowship from the *Oxford American* magazine, Brown lives in Gambier, Ohio, and teaches at Kenyon College, where she is the *Kenyon Review* Fellow in Poetry.

Selected Bibliography
Poems: *The Virginia State Colony for Epileptics and Feebleminded* (2017);
co-authored with Susannah Nevison, *In the Field Between Us* (2020). Essays: *Places I've Taken My Body* (2020).

THE CENTRAL VIRGINIA TRAINING CENTER
formerly The Virginia State Colony for Epileptics and Feebleminded

Whatever it is—
home or hospital,
graveyard or asylum,
government facility or great
tract of land slowly ceding
itself back to dust—

its church is a low-slung brick box
with a single window,
a white piece of plywood
labeled chapel, and a locked door.

Whatever it is,
my mother and I ride along
its red roads in February
with the windows down:
this place looks lived in,
that one has stiff, gray curtains
in the window, a roof caving in.

We see a small group moving
in the channel between one building
and the next, bowing in an absent wind.

He is in a wheelchair, she is stumbling,
pushing a pram from decades ago,
coal black and wrong. There is no way
it holds a baby. Behind them,
a few more shuffling bodies in coats.

I am my own kind of damaged there,
looking out the right-hand window.
Spastic, palsied and off-balance,
I'm taking crooked notes about this place.

It is the land where he is buried, the place
she spent her whole life, the room
where they made it impossible
for her to have children.

It is the colony where he did not learn to read,
but did paint every single slat of fence
you see that shade of yellow.

The place she didn't want to leave
when she finally could,
because she'd lived there fifty years,
and couldn't drive a car, or remember
the outside, or trust anyone
to touch her gently.

And, by some accident of luck or grace,
some window less than half a century wide,
it is my backyard but not what happened
to my body—

2017

LABOR

If you have the body for it, you're bound for the fields
to pick strawberries and coax the milk from cows,
or hired out to make baking powder biscuits and gravy,
to sweep floors and wash and fold a stranger's clothes.
You come back on a truck after sunset, raw and ragged, covered
in flour, tobacco, or clay. You come back bone-tired and bruised,
burned dead out and ready to be shut away. You sleep.

I know all this from stories; I do not have the body for it.
I do not go to the fields, or the barns, or the parlors of other folks' houses.
I wake at sunrise when they wake the rest, lie in bed
til somebody hauls me out and puts me by the window. Lord, I know
to want to work's a foolish thing to those who've got a body built for working.

I was as close to born here as you can get, brought twisted and mewling
to the gates and left. Since then, I am one long echo of somebody else's life.
Every understanding that I have is scrap, is shard, is secondhand.

> *Distance:* the space between the porch railing
> and the rise of the blue ridge

> *Water:* what comes from a bucket to my body on Sundays;
> what I open my mouth for, morning and night.

> *Sex:* The days the girls come back smelling of whiskey,
> snuff, and sweat, and something sharp.

2017

PRAYER FOR THE WRETCHED AMONG US

I.

Always they tell you to go
where God calls you.

What they don't say is that, sometimes,
God will call you to the wilderness,

gesture toward the trees, and then
hang back and wave you on alone.

This is how I wound up granting absolution
to low-grade idiots and the worn-out women

who turn them over in bed at night and,
at dawn, go home to their own families,

try not to think of ghosts
wasting away in this world.

II.

You are not supposed to be afraid of sinners.
You should take off your shoes and give them

to the wretched and the damned.
Hold out your hand to every girl

even if she seems more animal,
statue, or remnant of plague

than lost disciple. But,
do the children of God really lose

their eyes in the backs of their heads,
and swallow their own tongues in church?

III.

I should think of her as an infant,
a baby who is saved, although

she cannot say God's name
or even understand it.

But her knees, drawn up in the washtub,
tower past her chin. I pour

Holy water from a chipped blue pitcher,
cannot call up a prayer.

IV.

I'm glad for the twenty miles I drive
over the mountains each week,

for the latched red gate
at the mouth of Colony Road,

for the gloves I wear on days
I have to give last rites in the infirmary.

My wife is pregnant.
I am looking into the mouth of a nightmare.

Driving home in the dark,
I beg forgiveness

and louder, for protection
and the distance to forget.

2017

THE CONVULSIONS CHOIR

They did not build
the church
for us.

I overheard one night nurse
talking to another.
They meant it for the staff

as a refuge
from the stench,
the idiot, & the insane.

They meant: you will need God
more than ever
in this place.

After all,
we are a whole host of reasons
to stop believing in anything.

I am the worst thing
the reasoned world
has wrought,

> *an otherwise lovely girl*
> *daily visited by radical disorder*
> *they say spawns somewhere*
>
> *quiet & foaming*
> *in the wounded matter*
> *of my body & my brain.*

Sundays, we are allowed in the chapel
for an hour in the morning
after the men have prayed & gone.

There are too many bodies for the pews,
so those who can all gather in the back
like starlings stunned after a storm.

I'd like to take the hands of the other
epileptic girls & lead them
up toward the altar,

humming & weaving
our arms together
like chains.

> *I wonder if, in concert,*
> *we could call it up like hymns,*
> *like speaking in tongues.*
>
> *We could lie down & demand*
> *to be raptured, or healed, to return*
> *to safer bodies, or to dust.*

As the weeks I'm here
grow achingly
to months & years

I make an outside world
of the space between
my bones.

They did not build
the church
for us.

But they leave us
alone inside it,
bar the door.

2017

Maryann Corbett
(1950)

Maryann Corbett was born in Washington, DC, and raised in Arlington and McLean, Virginia. She attended The College of William and Mary and, shortly after graduating, married John Corbett; they both began graduate school at the University of Minnesota in the Fall of 1972, where she studied medieval literature and linguistics. In 1981, she received her doctorate, and she then worked for thirty-four-and-a-half years as a language specialist for the Office of the Revisor of Statutes for the Minnesota Legislature, retiring in 2016.

Although she did not begin writing poetry until 2006, Corbett has since published books of great quality with great frequency, quickly establishing herself, in Charles Martin's words, as "a poet and translator of remarkable accomplishment." Often beginning with incidents of daily life, her poems are deepened and enriched by the poet's long study of languages and literatures of the past, especially of the medieval and Renaissance periods, and by her aptitude for traditional verse forms, both those of the more common variety and rarer forms such as alliterative hemistichs, the *bouts-rimés*, the pantoum, and the Sapphic strophe. As Peter Campion has noted, "What makes Maryann Corbett such a rare, excellent writer must be her talent for weaving together various artistic impulses, so that her poems often sound both traditional and brand new, both humorous and serious, both worldly-wise and, as John Keats once put it, 'capable of being in uncertainties.'" Indeed, her work is informed by abiding tensions between Art and Nature, myth and fact, Time Present and Time Past, often relying upon her keen eye for detail and polyglot wordplay to achieve resolution with, as George David Clark puts it, an "exquisite, seemingly effortless grace."

Corbett is the author of two chapbooks and six full-length collections. Her work has won the Willis Barnstone Translation Prize (2009) and the Richard Wilbur Award (2014), and it appears in periodicals such as *32 Poems*, *The Best American Poetry*, *Birmingham Poetry Review*, *Ecotone*, *Literary Imagination*, and *PN Review*. Currently, she lives in St. Paul, Minnesota, with her husband.

Selected Bibliography
Breath Control (2012); *Credo for the Checkout Line in Winter* (2013); *Mid Evil* (2015); *Street View* (2017); *In Code* (2020); *The O in the Air* (2023).

NORTHEAST DIGS OUT FROM RECORD SNOWFALL

All up and down the coast, where Saturday
a generous snow came down, an ancient magic
appears this morning: every hack reporter
in every local rag now lifts the lyre
in lieu of pad and pencil. In New York,
it is a *milk-white morning*; snow transforms
the *straw-drab landscapes into winter postcards.*
Southward the mood is darker: *like a cloak
of madness* falls the snow, *like one of those
quiet obsessions you read about in stories.*
Figure and trope and image sift, drift over
the dailiness of the papers. Even where
the gods are feebler, on the weather page,
the lyric muse now takes the words by storm:
fierce winds and *dazzling whiteness, thigh-deep drifts,*
adjectives blowing thick and piling fast,
and under everything the sonorous meter
of radios intoning cancellations.
Those few lost souls with no poetic spark
wander the parks and murmur, staring upward,
"so quiet" and *"so lovely,"* and their awe
is duly reported, being perhaps the news
most worth reporting: beauty changes us,
calling up wonder from our deepest selves
to its right place, page one, above the fold.

2013

AIRHEADS

These past few days, our local air
displays its moves with floating fuzz:
cottonwood seed *scintillulas*[2]
accost my nostrils, haunt my hair.
They dance like Salome; they tease
with half-cracked helices of flight.
Waffling at each offered breeze,
fluff-head flecks, electron-light,
ride downdrafts like adagio rain—
the next half-second, loft again,
jumping at every chance to shirk
the settling down, the rooted work.
Bad moves, but just how I behave.
The weighty efforts that might save
my soul, my health, my solvency
I balk at, loving faddish stuff—
the fizz of tabloid and TV,
light music, frothy poetry—
composing life from airhead fluff.
No hundredfold of yield is found
from seed that never hits the ground,
so I take comfort when I see
white seed-fuzz piling up in grass,
brought down to earth by modest mass,
a ratio that pleases me:
some gravitas, much levity.

2013

---

2 A *scintillula* is a "little spark" in Latin. Cf. the English "scintilla" and "scintillate."

Historic District, Walking Garden Tour[3]

Tour the houses and gardens of historic Summit and Crocus Hill!
Talk with owners about preservation challenges. Tickets on sale now.
Proceeds to Summit Hill Association.

The porta-potties, set among the trees—
old elms, still dying off by slow degrees—
dispel illusions: no, we are not *guests*.
Invasive species, horticultural pests,
we let the greeters take our ticket stubs.
They flash the florid smiles of garden clubs.

These houses, treasures of the Gilded Age,
stand open to our gawking. Russian sage
drifts gauzily about a Roman arch.
Peer down a colonnade; step to a porch
tipsy with time warp, wound in rose-cane wreaths.
Old money is the sharp perfume this breathes.

By boxwood aisles (a century to grow them)
owners are grandly framed, so that we know them
and listen. This is one: the pencil skirt,
the manicure too delicate for dirt,
the mouth well-versed in families, classes, orders,
intoning to us in the dahlia borders

her burden: to maintain the grand façades
of Gilbert, Johnston, Richardson, the gods
of the Beaux-Arts, whose architectural creed
stands on the ground of nineteenth-century greed.
Guidebooks lapse into silence on the sins
that undergird their granite disciplines:

---

3   "While the James J. Hill House is not part of the annual Summit Avenue tour, its history, and
Hill's, lie behind this poem." – Corbett's note.

the dark red sandstone brooding on the hill
over the history of a steel-spiked will
that built and built and never had enough—
a public treasure now, it rules the bluff
and makes us marvel at our rush to own
the memory of the men it turned to stone.

Which we preserve, the robber baron's guilt
being gilded by the loveliness he built.
As for a feast day, every year we come
to hear the engines of our envy hum,
sighing for beauties, knowing what they meant.
Not quite complicit. Not quite innocent.

2017

DEFENDING VERONESE[4]

"Feast in the House of Levi," ca. 1573, formerly titled
"Last Supper"

I.

What has he done, poor terrified *pittore*,[5]
to end up hauled before this stern tribunal?
He's painted the Last Supper as the glory

of Venice. Sculpted sight lines into archways,
pigments into marble colonnades,
costume, color, and sweep into the marches

of banqueters, gesticulating servants,
a liveried dwarf, a cat who bats a bone—
just there, below the lace edge of the linens—

---

4 "In 1573, Veronese was called before the Inquisition on a charge of heresy to answer why he
had included jesters, soldiers, animals, and other frivolities at the Last Supper." – Corbett's note.
5 "Painter" (Italian).

a feast for the eyes, for the refectory wall
of the rich house that paid well to enjoy it,
the monastery of Saints John and Paul.

How, in an eyeblink, old men's views can change!
All art's upended. Now they're blasphemies,
those drunkards, dwarfs, and soldiers he's arranged

for drama. Now they mock the sacred setting
where all of Europe's staged an argument.
And so our Paolo stands stiff-legged, sweating

answers, babbling, barely making sense.
Artists, he blurts, *use license, just the same
as poets and madmen.* This is his best defense:

cloudy unknowing. He'll slither free of blame
by promising repentance, and he'll change
nothing at all except the picture's name.

For none but the inquisitors mistook
his real intentions. It's his light that's prayer.
Color and movement: prayer. To make us *look*

is what he wants. No vexed theology
of sacrament, of *hoc est enim corpus*,[6]
challenges those who stroll the Gallerie,

only the gorgeous tumult of that sky.

II.

And this is grace. This is the catechesis
we need now, for the kind of sight we work with
here, where the world kabooms. Where all we see is

---

6 Abbreviation of the Latin phrase "hoc est enim Corpus Meum," or "For this is My Body":
Christ's words at The Last Supper, repeated during the Eucharistic Liturgy of each Roman Catholic
Mass.

each day's amazement blasting at our eyes,
we need to master finding the still place,
seeing through bloom and buzz to mysteries

where not quite at the focal point, the Holy,
wordless and calm, waits now for our attention.
That gesture that saves lives, that food of souls,

keeps low to the table, and the troubled face
is lit with a nimbus we have to squint to see,
framed as it is by backlit cumulus

at twilight, hung above the port of Venice.

2017

Prophesying to the Breath

I'm tired of it, this labored breathing. Tired
of phlegm and coughing, and the fight for air,
bent double on the landing of a stair,
in wheezing gasps where nothing is inspired.
Tired of the silence next to me in bed
when measured snoring suddenly goes still,
of counting a nervous *one, two, three* until
it starts itself again. Tired of my dread.
I want it back: the confidence in air—
ruah, pneuma, spiritus[7]—the breath
that stirs the vocal folds of nuns in choir.
The breath that Is. The sound of something there
guiding this gusty round of birth and death.
The rush of driving wind. The tongues of fire.[8]

2014

---

7 Words meaning "wind, breath, or spirit" in Hebrew, Greek, and Latin, respectively.
8 Cf. Acts 2:3.

STAGING DIRECTIONS

Their revels now are ended. These, their agents,
        powdered of face,
voguish of dress, stand sizing up the place.
        Patience.

        Buyers in twos and threes
must swagger through these rooms, seeing themselves
brilliant against the beige neutralities
of freshly painted walls and curio'd shelves

these sorcerers will conjure. Yard-sale youth,
ragged and randy past, begone. Away,
sticky mementos of the childish truth,
forgotten glitter and misshapen clay.

Old chafings, be undone in this chastisement of their peace,
        this cleansing
        stripping-away of dross, flensing
of what they were. Let this be the release

        that gentles them away.
Let the house sell and settle, and the debt
be null. Let them become the empty set
        for someone else's play.

2017

Sarah Cortez (1950)

Sarah Cortez's gritty and sensual poems are grounded in her day-to-day experience of policing the streets of Houston, Texas. Naomi Shihab Nye has praised their "tough muscles, neat lines, and rippling visceral imagery." A relative latecomer to writing, Cortez grew up in Houston. She majored in psychology and religion at Rice University and earned a Master of Arts degree in classical studies at the University of Texas, and then taught Latin at St. Agnes Academy in Houston for two years before earning a Master of Science degree in Accountancy from the University of Houston. During her sixteen-year corporate career, she began taking writing classes at the University of Houston. A later switch into law enforcement, which she calls "the best thing I've ever done," found her already a published author. After almost six years of full-time policing, she became a reserve officer with one of the Harris County Constable's offices and accepted a visiting scholar position at the University of Houston's Center for Mexican-American Studies. She has gone on to teach writing in multiple genres to students ranging from third graders to senior citizens, and she has served on the Board of the Texas Institute of Letters, an organization devoted to promoting literacy and recognizing literary achievement.

Cortez was awarded the 1999 PEN Texas Literary Award for Poetry, and in 2003 she was chosen by the then-mayor of Houston, Bill White, to write and deliver a poem for his inauguration. The United Nations invited Ms. Cortez to compose and deliver a poem for the Eighth Permanent Forum on Indigenous Issues. One of her poems was also chosen for the national "Poetry in Motion" program. Cortez currently works as a freelance writer, teacher, and reserve deputy in Harris County, Texas. Cortez has edited numerous anthologies. Her spiritual memoir in poetry and prose, *Walking Home: Growing Up Hispanic in Houston,* was praised by the *Houston Chronicle* as "a love letter to the city of Houston."

Selected Bibliography
Poems: *How to Undress a Cop* (2000); *Cold Blue Steel* (2013); *Against Sky's Warm Belly: New and Selected Poems* (2016). Mixed-genre memoir: *Walking Home: Growing Up Hispanic in Houston* (2012). Essays: *Tired, Hungry, and Standing in One Place for Twelve Hours: Essential Cop Essays* (2018).

LINGO

This is how it goes
when you're dating
a cop.

You say, "Will you be home for dinner?"
He says, "Negative."

You say, "Do you like this dress?"
and he says, "It's a good visual."

"Face to face" is a meeting,
not a kiss or a snuggle.
"Fuck you" means hello.
"To dust" is to kill.

On Valentine's when I say
my bra size is 34B
saying the "B" twice, so
the embarrassing "D" cup
won't be purchased, he
says, "Oh, yeah, 34 BRAVO."
I smile, hoping he'll find
a color lace I don't already have
under my own police uniform.

What isn't said is I love
you. Don't get shot tonight
on shift by a cop-hater. Don't die
before I die, alone
in an alleyway or on a bright street
in widening pools of blood.

2000

Tu Negrito[9]

She's got to bail me out,
he says into the phone outside the holding cell.
She's going there tomorrow anyway for Mikey.
Tell her she's got to do this for me.

He says into the phone outside the holding cell,
Make sure she listens. Make her feel guilty, man.
Tell her she's got to do this for me.
She can have all my money, man.

Make sure she listens. Make her feel guilty, man.
Tell her she didn't bail me out the other times.
She can have all my money, man.
She always bails out Mikey.

Tell her she didn't bail me out the other times.
I don't got no one else to call, cousin.
She always bails out Mikey.
Make sure you write all this down, cousin.

I don't got no one else to call, cousin.
I really need her now.
Make sure you write all this down, cousin.
Page her. Put in code 333. That's me.

I really need her now.
Write down "Mommie." Change it from "Mom."
Page her. Put in code 333. That's me.
Write down "*Tu Negrito*." Tell her I love her.

Write down "Mommie." Change it from "Mom."
I'm her littlest. Remind her.
Write down "*Tu Negrito*." Tell her I love her.
She's got to bail me out.

2000

---

9 "Your little black one."

A Certain Kind of Case

My buddy Danny says, "You can't work
those kinds of cases your whole career. It changes
you. You have to watch videos.
Hours and hours. You have to understand

how they think." I realize I'd never thought
of it—who worked those cases, who
they went home to and what their wives fixed
for dinner. How they fell asleep, still thinking

about those tapes. Danny shakes his head
back and forth, disbelieving. "It takes at least five
years for an investigator to get good. You have to learn
certain terms they use among each other. Once

we did a search warrant at a pedophile's house. Less than
five minutes after the tape's delivery and it was
already in his VCR. Trash knee-deep inside. Piled high
in every room of his house, except the closet

where he kept his films and books. Totally
clean. Dust-free. Labeled by category in precise block
letters. Alphabetized like a library. We had to wear
overalls, gloves, and boots to walk through
half-eaten rotting food in wrappers."

2000

ROSIE WORKING PLAIN CLOTHES

She's a dish—that Rosie.
Half Mexican; half Irish.
Green eyes backed by a hell of a temper,
perfect peach skin and black curly hair.
Large breasts.

Rosie and I were standing together
in the females' locker room and,
you understand, I wasn't really looking at her chest,
but out of the corner of my eyes, I saw, I swear
to God, I saw her pull out from deep,
deep in her cleavage in the center of her pink lacy bra,
I saw her pull out an aluminum-finish,
eight inch long, nine millimeter, semi-automatic.
Then she pulled out one set of heavy-duty,
brushed stainless, Smith and Wesson handcuffs,
each side dangling from the other like an earring.
And then she pulled out her black plastic beeper,
and, my God, by this time I was staring. Flat-out
admiration. Complete and total fascination.
Oh, yes, that Rosie, she's quite a cop!

2000

Kate Daniels (1953)

Kate Daniels was born and raised in Richmond, Virginia. She attended the University of Virginia and was the first member of her family to graduate from college, earning both a BA and an MA in English Literature before going on to Columbia University, where she earned an MFA. Subsequently a Bunting Fellow at Harvard University, Daniels devoted her early career to studying the poet Muriel Rukeyser, ultimately editing a selection of Rukeyser's poems entitled *Out of Silence* (TriQuarterly Books, 1992). Daniels has taught at the University of Massachusetts-Amherst, Louisiana State University, Bennington College, and Wake Forest University. Formerly the Director of Creative Writing at Vanderbilt University, she is currently the Edward Mims Professor of English *Emerita* at Vanderbilt. She has also taught at the Washington Baltimore Center for Psychoanalysis. Her work has been widely published and anthologized in periodicals such as *Best American Poetry*, *Five Points*, *New England Review*, *The Oxford American*, *The Southern Review*, and *The Virginia Quarterly Review*.

The recipient of numerous awards—including a Guggenheim Fellowship, a Pushcart Prize, and the Hanes Award for Poetry from the Fellowship of Southern Writers—Daniels was awarded the prestigious Agnes Lynch Starrett Poetry Prize for her first collection of poems, *The White Wave*. Of her first book, Pulitzer Prize-winner Stanley Kunitz wrote, "Kate Daniels' dramatic imagination creates a world for us that is vividly, sometimes painfully real, with a bold clarity of detail," and National Book Award-winner Gerald Stern added, "Only deep feeling, and the courage and humanity to confront that feeling, could produce such clarity." Both statements have proven apt. With great "courage and humanity" Daniels has written about a wide variety of subjects, including childhood, gender roles, racial politics, mythology, theology, parenthood, aging, and addiction. However, for all their variety, her poems consistently display a dazzling and multifaceted clarity, resisting the temptation to oversimplify and thus distort reality. Equally capable of crafting chiseled lyrics and magnificent longer poems (such as those found in the brilliant *Four Testimonies*, represented in this anthology by a single excerpt due to considerations of space), Daniels consistently "captures the stuff we humans are made of—dark and light—the nitty-gritty truths of flesh and blood, sweat and tears," as Pulitzer Prize-winner Yusef Komunyakaa writes, revealing over and again "the painful shape of truth beneath real skin."

Selected Bibliography
Poems: *The White Wave* (1984); *The Niobe Poems* (1988); *Four Testimonies* (1998); *A Walk in Victoria's Secret* (2010); *In the Months of My Son's Recovery* (2019); Memoir: *Slow Fuse of the Possible* (2022).

The Playhouse

My dolls came alive in it,
all of them whining in unison.
And there was a pink curtain.
I'd part it and see your hand
flailing at the bedroom window,
beckoning me in.

But my dolls needed me, too,
wetting their little diapers,
mewing *Ma-Ma* whenever I thumped
their stomachs.
I pretended my hair was long
like yours, draped a black towel
over my head and nuzzled the dollies
till it fell over them
covering their faces.

Each of us in our houses:
I thought of you combing your hair
before the mirror,
chatting about men who had loved you,
how my father was a fool,
what you wished you had done.

I never knew why you wanted me.
I was alone out there. I loved you
away from the spectre of your black hair
gleaming in the mirror, your lovely face
talking to itself.

1984

DOGTOWN, 1957

In the piney, pink stria of summer morning skies, we awoke
to the muted, moan-like howling of the hungry redbones
locked in their chain-link compounds. They lived their lives
like that: locked in wire cages until released to hunt, fragmented
images of earlier expeditions flickering in and out of whatever
consciousness they possessed, exciting them to live. Maybe
somewhere in their genetic memories there existed remnant
images of the fleeing slaves their ancestors had pursued north
through the boggy bottoms of the Dismal Swamp to Dogtown,
where freed slaves and poor whites had subsisted for a century,
economically bonded in perpetuity to the gentrified bastards
living north of the river, who valued nothing more than saving
the fabled cobblestones of Monument Avenue from urban renewal.
There, on that broad swath of grassy boulevard, the horsebacked
Confederate generals, deceased in war, cantered statically
through eternity, unaware their dream was dead.

And here in Dogtown, across the river from that genteel boulevard
with its antique mansions and art museums, with its tennis courts
and flower gardens, we didn't seem to be going anywhere either.
We arose each day and heard the members of our family
clambering past each other for access to the solitary bath
that lacked a tub, our unkempt toenails clicking on the scarred wood floors.
No one spoke, but we could hear the thwonging hiss of my father's
early morning piss throughout that house, and the foamy scratch
of my uncle's razor on his chin as he shaved around his cigarette.
Already, the day's allotment of acrid smoke and malodorous saucers
of stubbed-out butts had begun to mount. The smell stuck in our hair,
in our clothes, turning them rancid. Someone switched on an AM radio.
Someone stirred brown-black granules of instant coffee in a cup of boiling
    water.
Then, among the ashtrays and the matchbooks on the table top,
we poured out bowls of cold cereal from paper boxes, and fell into them,
lapping the milk like famished creatures. Outside, the other
creatures shook the fencing of their pens, hurling themselves

full-length on the chain link walls while we screamed at them
to hush. But they were dogs, and knew no better. Undeterred
by our demand for silence, they went on howling, mindlessly, inside their
   cages.

2010

GETTING CLEAN

i

You can boil yourself down
to the rudiments, all the way
to the very bottom, and sit there
pruning yourself to the compact form
of a bouillon cube, its salty bite
stuffed tight inside, and *still*
be suffused with mindless craving ...

ii

On the bad days, he said, *before*
I even get out of bed I have to pray.

I asked him if he would mind
telling me what he prayed for.

I just say, "Help. Help me.
Could you help me get out of bed ..."

iii

In the middle of the meeting, an old-timer suddenly
yelled out, "Sit down and suffer, and shut the hell up."

iv

Hate to tell you:
the torment might
not dissipate. And
though you think
it might have sunk,
don't be fooled. It's
not a ship. Still alive,
still growing. After
treatment, if you're
lucky, slightly shrunk.

v

Shrunk or unshrunk,
the new thinking says
that craving lives on
hoarding its power.

Even the addicts
who are atheists
learn this lesson:
There is something
bigger than they are,
and unlike them,
it lives forever.

2019

NIOBE OF THE PAINTING

—after Maurice-Denis's *La petite fille à la robe rouge*

The girl in the red dress
is coming apart. Nothing
is holding her together
but imagination.

She's hurrying, but it's too late.
The gun has just gone off,
the water has already risen,
the car has skidded into the curve.
Once, she might have made it,
but now she knows too much
for eagerness or optimism.
Her heart is old
though her step is light.
All that remains is something
civilized: polite
consideration. So she's hurrying
out of the picture to spare us the sight
of her indifferent surrender.
She knows it will happen to us, too.
She knows we are all coming apart,
that nothing holds anyone together
but imagination, pretense,
a rare day of good weather.

1988

READING A BIOGRAPHY OF THOMAS JEFFERSON
IN THE MONTHS OF MY SON'S RECOVERY

> Willpower is nothing. Morals is nothing. Lord, this is illness.
> —John Berryman

Because he bought the great swath of mucky swamp
And marshy wetland on the southern edge of the newborn nation,
Then let it alone, so it could fulminate, over time
Into its queer and patchwork, private self—

Because he forged a plowshare from paranoia
About the motivations of Napoleon, declining to incite
A war, and approved, instead, a purchase order—

Because he would have settled for New Orleans, but acquired
The whole thing anyway, through perseverance and hard
Bargaining, and not being too close with the government's money—

Because he bought it *all.*
                 A half million acres.

                          Sight unseen—

Because he loved great silences, and alligators, and bustling ports,
And unfettered access to commerce, and international
Trade, and bowery, stone-paved courtyards, noisy
With clattering palms, and formal drawing rooms
Cooled with high ceilings and shuttered windows, furnished
In the lush, upholstered styles of Louis Quinze. Because he valued
Imported wines and dark, brewed coffees, and had a tongue
That understood those subtle differences, but still succumbed,
Thrilled as a child by the strange, uncatalogued creatures that crawled
And swam and winged themselves through the unknown Territory—

Because of all this, I return thanks to Thomas Jefferson
For his flawed example of human greatness, for the mind-boggling
Diversity of Louisiana—birthplace of my second son,
13th of December 1990, the largest child delivered
                 to the state that day ...

      *

Can't help drawing back at how he lived in two minds
Because he was *of two minds* like a person
With old-time manic depression: the slaveholder
And the Democrat, the tranquil hilltop of Monticello,
And the ringing cobblestones of Paris, France. The white
Wife, and the concubine: enslaved and black ...

      *

Before he was my son, he was contained
Within a clutch of dangling eggs that waited,
All atremble, for his father's transforming glob
Of universal glue.

From the beginning—*before*
The beginning—before he had arranged
Himself into a fetal entity, and begun
Growing inside of me, he was endangered
By the mind-breaking molecules our ancestors
Hoarded, and passed forward in a blameless
Game of chance, shuffling the genes.

Even then, two minds circulated inside him,
Tantalizing a brand-new victim with generations
Of charged-up narratives of drugs and drink,
Of suicide and mania, of melancholic unmodulated
Moods, bedeviling distant aunts who died early,
And wild cousins who loved their night drives
On dark roads with doused headlights, speedometer
Straining to the arc of its limit, mothers who danced
On the dining room table, kicking aside the Thanksgiving
Turkey, carefully basted hours before.

We marveled at him in his bassinet—such
An unsoothable infant, so unreconciled to breathing
Oxygen, wearing a diaper, waiting for milk.
Still small and manageable at first. But whirling
Moods, baby-sized, and effervescent
As the liminal clouds of early spring, stalked him
Even then. Even then
                              This Thing stalked him
Threatening his freedom
                              And his right to self-rule.

        *

        We hold these truths to be self-evident, that all men
        are created equal, that they are endowed by their
        Creator with certain unalienable Rights, that among
        these are Life, Liberty and the pursuit of Happiness.
                —From the Declaration of Independence (1776)

Before we *were*
Ourselves he knew us. Explained us
To ourselves. Gave us a language whereby
We understood the restless grandiosities of our forebears,
And set us off on our well-trod path of personal
Liberty and greedy freedom-seeking. Minted the metaphors
We go on living by and misinterpreting, and clobbering
Over the heads of the rest of the world—Still,
His language stirs me up. Still, I believe
He was a great man, and seek in the painful
Contradictions of his personal life and public
Service, ongoing signs for how to live
In *this* strange era.

*

I know of no safe depository of the ultimate powers
of society but the people themselves. And if we
think them not enlightened enough to exercise
their control with a wholesome discretion,
the remedy is not to take it from them,
but to inform their discretion by education ...
            —From a Letter to W.C. Jarvis (1820)

Once more, we drive our son to the treatment center,
And sign him in, and watch him stripped of identity
And privacy. Shoelaces and cigarettes. Cell phone.
A dog-eared novel by Cormac McCarthy. A plastic bag
Stuffed with things we take away with us, and weep over,
Driving home. He has lost the safe depository of himself.
Is dispossessed. Is lacking any wholesome discretion
On his own behalf. Indicted by genetics, disempowered
By blood, how should we school him, except by love
And psychotropic medications?

*

Flight of ideas and verbal grandiosity:
Imaginary master of vast terrains, teeming
With fanciful creatures and fearsome weather:
A Louisiana Territory of a child's mind
Born there, after all, its doors and windows
Propped open to admit the gorgeous scenes
Of extreme weather, thriving in the rapid cycles
Of tropical heat, the coloratura of radical sunsets,
The tympanic symphonies of downpours
That dampened every day, and then were
Scorched dry by the blistering sun. Early
Symptoms we overlooked, and nurtured instead
As precocious tendencies of a burgeoning poet
Or a future president ...

*

The man must be a prodigy who can retain
his manners and morals undepraved by such
circumstances [as those of slavery].
—FROM *Notes on the State of Virginia* (1787)

In the long nights when I can't sleep,
When anxiety courses through my body,
Racheting up to a stiff rod of fear and dread
I feel impaled upon, I sometimes let my mind
Drift to Thomas Jefferson and his famous
Inconsistencies ... Here he is, tranquilly
Trotting through the bracing sunlight
Of national history, all long bones and red hair,
The eloquent incitements of his discourse scrolling
Out the documents that determined our fate.
But there he is at night, other mind in ascendance,
Tying shut the bed-curtains of a lover he inventoried
Among his personal property. With whom he made
Six children. Though he legally "owned" her.
And then "owned" them. His very own—
His sons and daughters ...

The way that two things can coexist without
Canceling each other out—how did he live
Like that? *How does my own son live like that?*
As a schoolchild longs for certainty, I crave
An answer, and sometimes hold my two hands up
To weigh the *yes* against the *no*, slavery
In one hand, freedom in the other: a tiny exercise
In bipolarity that never helps.

      *

Sometimes it helps to latch on
To someone else's vision
In a crisis—the way I did
At Monticello, so long ago,
Stumbling among the rain-slicked
Bricks of orderly paths. Working-class girl
In cheap shoes and plastic glasses,
Bad teeth. Terrified by the new world
Of the mind I'd entered. From the strict
Arrangements and smoothed-out edges
Of all those interwoven pavers someone baked
From clay, carted there, laid out by hand,
Brick by brick by brick, I carved a small sanity
Where I could rest. And read.

      *

I cannot live without books, he wrote.
And so gave permission for a kind of life
Previously unimaginable: this life I live now—
Soothing myself and seeking comprehension
Among my many volumes.

                        2019

LATE APOLOGY TO DORIS HASKINS

Come in, lone black girl, and sit among us.
And if there are twenty whites and only
one of you? No matter. New laws say
it must be so, and that we should
ignore the inequality that clouds
our visions of each other.

                              And so—
we sit here through the dragging day,
clock hands lagging maddeningly,
lessons sidelined, watching you
not watching us—your head
with its plethora of plastic barrettes,
your neat white socks creaming
your ankles. We circle you, sniffing.
And no one dares to enter the restroom
after you, perchance to occupy
the cool white seat you might have sat
upon for brief relief. And not one
of us will march beside you to the lunchroom
or the asphalt field where we play our games.
Each day, we hope the threats of bombs your presence
summons to what used to be our all-white school
will come again. For hours, then, we'll be out of class,
and free to wallow on the green front lawn, ignoring you
sitting off to the side, alone as usual, your plaid-skirted lap
filled with the torn-up blooms of buttercups.

We don't know why you are among us, or what
your presence means, or why we must attend
the mystery you make—a little girl who's more or less
identical to us despite the tales our parents tell.
Evenings, we watch them demonstrating on the TV news
in long, hot lines outside the board of education.
We read their signs and memorize the close-ups
of their faces twisted up with hate.

We watch them, as we eat our meals
on trays before the screen.

                       Your family
must watch them, too, before they kill the set
and send you off to bathe and pray and sleep.
Perhaps your mother stands, like mine,
late into the night, pressing flat the wrinkles
in your skirt with a hot iron, her mind
crowded with old terror she no longer
has the energy to fight. In the morning,
she will send her only daughter—a girl of ten—
forward into new light to vanquish it at last.
As will mine send forth *her* only daughter
to face the other side of your mother's terror.
And we will sit beside each other, Doris, gleaming
in our brand new classroom, sanctioned by the law,
spelling unfamiliar words, and calculating
complicated sums.

                               2010

War Photograph

A naked child is running
along the path toward us,
her arms stretched out,
her mouth open,
the world turned to trash
behind her.

She is running from the smoke
and the soldiers, from the bodies
of her mother and little sister
thrown down into a ditch,

from the blown-up bamboo hut
from the melted pots and pans.
And she is also running from the gods
who have changed the sky to fire
and puddled the earth with skin and blood.
She is running—my god—to us,
10,000 miles away,
reading the caption
beneath her picture
in a weekly magazine.
All over the country
we're feeling sorry for her
and being appalled at the war
being fought in the other world.
She keeps on running, you know,
after the shutter of the camera
clicks. She's running to us.
For how can she know,
her feet beating a path
on another continent?
How can she know
what we really are?
From the distance, we look
so terribly human.

1988

Prayer to the Muse of Ordinary Life

I seek it in the steamy odor
of the iron pressing cotton shirts
in the heat of a summer afternoon,
in my daughter's ear, the warm pink
cone, curling inward. I seek it
in the dusty circles of the ceiling fan,
the kitchen counter with its painted shells

from Hilton Head, the creaking boards
in the bedroom floor, the coconut
cookies in the blue glass jar.
The hard brown knob of nutmeg nestled
in the silver grater and the lemon
yogurt that awaits. I seek it not
in books but in my life inscribed
in two brief words—*mother, wife*
—the life I live as mistress of an unkempt
manse, volunteer at firstborn's
school, alternate Wednesdays'
aide at youngest's nursery, billpayer,
laundress, cook, shrewd purchaser of mid-
priced minivan. I seek it
in the strophes of a life
like this, wondering what
it could be like, its narratives
drawn from the nursery and playpen,
its images besmirched with vomitus
and shit. The prayer I pray is this:

If you are here,
where are you?
If you exist,
what are you?
I beg you
to reveal yourself.
I will not judge,
I am not fancy.
My days are filled
with wiping noses
and bathing bottoms,
with boiling pots
of cheese-filled pasta
for toothless mouths
while reading Rilke,[10]
weeping.

---

10 Rainer Maria Rilke [1975–1926]: a Bohemian-Austrian poet, considered by many the greatest German-language poet of the twentieth century.

My life is broken
into broken pieces.
The fabric is rent.
Daily, I roll
the stone away
but all is dark
inside, unchanged.
The miracle has not
happened yet.

If you are anywhere
nearby, show me
anything at all
to prove you do exist:
a poem in a small, soiled
nightie, a lyric
in the sandbox voices
raised in woe.

Release a stanza
from the sink's hot suds
where dirty dishes grow.
Seal a message inside:
encourage me
to hold on.
Inform me
in detail
exactly how to do it.

1998

Carolyn Forché (1950)

Poet, translator, memoirist, and human rights activist Carolyn Forché coined the term "poetry of witness" to describe poems that explore the world's atrocities and their effects. In her groundbreaking international anthology, *Against Forgetting: Twentieth-Century Poetry of Witness,* Forché collected the work of poets who had endured exile, war, torture, imprisonment, and censorship. Of her own poetry, Derek Walcott has said that it "will continue to haunt the future . . . and during whatever fresh horror our century will repeat each morning, [condemns] them not with dialectic, but by the ironic serenity of beauty."

Forché was born in Detroit to a tool-and-die-maker father and a journalist mother. She earned a BA in Creative Writing at Michigan State University and an MFA at Bowling Green State University in 1975. A year later, her first book, *Gathering the Tribes,* was chosen by Stanley Kunitz for the prestigious Yale Series of Young Poets Award, and Forché traveled to Spain to translate the works of exiled Salvadorian poet Claribel Alegría. In 1978 Forché received a Guggenheim Fellowship that brought her to El Salvador where she witnessed that nation's civil war and became a human rights activist and reporter. These experiences, as well as subsequent travel in South Africa, fueled her interest in local revolutionary movements and the effects of US diplomacy around the world, an interest that in turn would shape her own poetry. Forché's second book, *The Country Between Us,* received the 1981 Lamont poetry selection and went on to become a bestseller. Her memoir, *What You Have Heard Is True: A Memoir of Witness and Resistance,* takes its title from her most famous poem, "The Colonel."

Forché has translated the poetry of Georg Trakl, Robert Desnos, and Mahmoud Darwish and has received fellowships from the Lannan Foundation, the National Endowment for the Arts, and the Academy of American Poets as well as the Edita and Ira Morris Hiroshima Foundation Award. She has taught at numerous universities, including the University of Virginia, Skidmore College, Columbia University, George Mason University, and Georgetown University. She lives in Maryland with her husband, the photographer Harry Mattison.

Selected Bibliography

Poems: *Gathering the Tribes* (1976); *The Country Between Us* (1981); *The Angel of History* (1994); *Blue Hour* (2003); *In the Lateness of the World* (2020). Memoir: *What You Have Heard Is True: A Memoir of Witness and Resistance* (2020). As editor: *Against Forgetting: Twentieth-Century Poems of Witness* (1993).

THE MORNING BAKING

Grandma, come back, I forgot
How much lard for these rolls

Think you can put yourself in the ground
Like plain potatoes and grow in Ohio?
I am damn sick of getting fat like you

Think you can lie through your Slovak?
Tell filthy stories about the blood sausage?
Pish-pish nights at the virgin in Detroit?

I blame you raising me up for my Slav tongue
You beat me up out back, taught me to dance

I'll tell you I don't remember any kind of bread
Your wavy loaves of flesh
Stink through my sleep
The stars on your silk robes

But I'm glad I'll look when I'm old
Like a gypsy dusha[11] hauling milk

1976

EXPATRIATE

American life, you said, is not possible.
Winter in Syracuse, Trotsky pinned
to your kitchen wall, windows facing
a street, boxes of imported cigarettes.

---

11 soul.

The film *In the Realm of the Senses,*
and piles of shit burning and the risk
of having your throat slit. Twenty-year-old poet.
To be in love with some woman who cannot speak
English, to have her soften your back with oil
and beat on your mattress with grief and pleasure
as you take her from behind, moving beneath you
like the beginning of the world.
The black smell of death as blood and glass
is hosed from the street and the beggar holds
his diminishing hand to your face.
It would be good if you could wind up
in prison and so write your prison poems.
Good if you could marry the veiled face
and jeweled belly of a girl who could
cook Turkish meat, baste your body
with a wet and worshipful tongue.
Istanbul, you said, or *Serbia,* mauve
light and mystery and passing for other
than American, a *Kalashnikov*[12] over
your shoulder, spraying your politics
into the flesh of an enemy become real.
You have been in Turkey a year now.
What have you found? Your letters
describe the boring ritual of tea,
the pittance you are paid to teach
English, the bribery required for so much
as a postage stamp. Twenty-year-old poet,
Hikmet[13] did not choose to be Hikmet.

1981

---

12 automatic rifle.
13 Nâzim Hikmet, Turkish poet repeatedly arrested for his political beliefs.

Selective Service

We rise from the snow where we've
lain on our backs and flown like children,
from the imprint of perfect wings and cold gowns,
and we stagger together wine-breathed into town
where our people are building
their armies again, short years after
body bags, after burnings. There is a man
I've come to love after thirty, and we have
our rituals of coffee, of airports, regret.
After love we smoke and sleep
with magazines, two shot glasses
and the black and white collapse of hours.
In what time do we live that it is too late
to have children? In what place
that we consider the various ways to leave?
There is no list long enough
for a selective service card shriveling
under a match, the prison that comes of it,
a flag in the wind eaten from its pole
and boys sent back in trash bags.
We'll tell you. You were at that time
learning fractions. We'll tell you
about fractions. Half of us are dead or quiet
or lost. Let them speak for themselves.
We lie down in the fields and leave behind
the corpses of angels.

1981

The Colonel

What you have heard is true. I was in his house. His wife carried
a tray of coffee and sugar. His daughter filed her nails, his son went
out for the night. There were daily papers, pet dogs, a pistol on the
cushion beside him. The moon swung bare on its black cord over
the house. On the television was a cop show. It was in English.
Broken bottles were embedded in the walls around the house to
scoop the kneecaps from a man's legs or cut his hands to lace. On
the windows there were gratings like those in liquor stores. We had
dinner, rack of lamb, good wine, a gold bell was on the table for
calling the maid. The maid brought green mangoes, salt, a type of
bread. I was asked how I enjoyed the country. There was a brief
commercial in Spanish. His wife took everything away. There was
some talk then of how difficult it had become to govern. The parrot
said hello on the terrace. The colonel told it to shut up, and pushed
himself from the table. My friend said to me with his eyes: say
nothing. The colonel returned with a sack used to bring groceries
home. He spilled many human ears on the table. They were like
dried peach halves. There is no other way to say this. He took one
of them in his hands, shook it in our faces, dropped it into a water
glass. It came alive there. I am tired of fooling around he said. As
for the rights of anyone, tell your people they can go fuck them-
selves. He swept the ears to the floor with his arm and held the last
of his wine in the air. Something for your poetry, no? he said. Some
of the ears on the floor caught this scrap of his voice. Some of the
ears on the floor were pressed to the ground.

May 1978

1981

For the Stranger

Although you mention Venice
keeping it on your tongue like a fruit pit
and I say yes, perhaps Bucharest, neither of us
really knows. There is only this train
slipping through pastures of snow,
a sleigh reaching down
to touch its buried runners.
We meet on the shaking platform,
the wind's broken teeth sinking into us.
You unwrap your dark bread
and share with me the coffee
sloshing into your gloves.
Telegraph posts chop the winter fields
into white blocks, in each window
the crude painting of a small farm.
We listen to mothers scolding
children in English as if
we do not understand a word of it—
sit still, sit still.

There are few clues as to where
we are: the baled wheat scattered
everywhere like missing coffins.
The distant yellow kitchen lights
wiped with oil.
Everywhere the black dipping wires
stretching messages from one side
of a country to the other.
The men who stand on every border
waving to us.

Wiping ovals of breath from the windows
in order to see ourselves, you touch
the glass tenderly wherever it holds my face.
Days later, you are showing me

photographs of a woman and children
smiling from the windows of your wallet.

Each time the train slows, a man
with our faces in the gold buttons
of his coat passes through the cars
muttering the name of a city. Each time
we lose people. Each time I find you
again between the cars, holding out
a scrap of bread for me, something
hot to drink, until there are
no more cities and you pull me
toward you, sliding your hands
into my coat, telling me
your name over and over, hurrying
your mouth into mine.
We have, each of us, nothing.
We will give it to each other.

1981

John Foy (1960)

John Foy was born in New York City in 1960. He earned a BA in English from McGill University in Montreal before moving to Paris, where he spent six years working as an assistant editor and freelance writer for the *International Herald Tribune*. Upon returning to the United States, he earned an MFA from Columbia University in 1994. Between 1995 and 2000, he was the Berlitz Language School's Pedagogical Director for North America, and from 2000–2008 he worked for Bear Stearns, where he served as Managing Editor for High Yield and Emerging Market Research. From 2008, he worked as a financial editor for a Latin American investment bank.

Foy's poetry is characterized by "a delicate contrariety," an almost painterly counterpointing of painstakingly rendered detail with a most severe vision, in a manner at times reminiscent of Elizabeth Bishop or Robinson Jeffers. Some of his more recent poems also deploy the language of finance in ferocious satires combatting that grim vision of the world, which sees the human as a mere consumer or statistic lacking the illumination of any divine spark. As the accomplished poet-critic Adam Kirsch has written, Foy is a poet who "sees the dark and sees in the dark, with a clarity that few poets can achieve even in daylight." Indeed, Foy's verse often confronts those aspects of daily life typically consigned to the shadows for the sake of convenience or comfort.

And yet, in his resistance to the objectification of the human, Foy is also capable of reaching near-dizzying lyrical heights, and in many of his poems about family, friends, or creatures, he achieves, as Timothy Steele has noted, a profoundly humane "warmth and sympathy." Often magnanimous, and sometimes wounded by the world's cruelty, Foy's poetry nevertheless persists in its faithful and earnest rendering of contemporary experience. Foy has received both the New Criterion Poetry Prize and the Donald Justice Poetry Prize, and his work has appeared in periodicals such as *The Hopkins Review*, *The Hudson Review*, *Literary Matters*, *The New Criterion*, *The New Yorker*, *Poetry*, *Southwest Review*, and *The Yale Review*.

Selected Bibliography
Techne's Clearinghouse (2004); *Night Vision* (2016); *No One Leaves the World Unhurt* (2021).

Eucalyptus Trees

(Brejal, state of Rio de Janeiro)

Look how their longing has mastered them.
           Purged of every impulse
                      but the will to rise,

each a chancellor now,
           they tower single-mindedly
                      out along the road.

No doubting their affinity
           with whatever strives to disengage itself
                      from all those baser elements:

the riotous bamboo, the dutiful hedge,
           the coy azalea bush that casts
                      aspersions in the dirt.

These, the eucalyptus trees,
           avail themselves of the empyreal,
                      high tops tossed at altitudes

where only wind prevails
         —how pale and tenuous
                      their visible commitment to the earth.

No wonder, then, they leave behind
           the rougher skin, as contemplatives
                      let fall away the trappings of this world,

consigning to oblivion
           the shirts they'll never use again.
                      Stripped thus, the eucalyptus trees ascend,

saudade[14] their abstract attribute,
         a yearning for the spires
                  they wish they could become.

---

14 *Saudade* is a Portuguese word meaning "melancholy" or "nostalgia" or "yearning."

It's a predilection for air and light
    that keeps them reaching
        after higher signatures,

a time unheard of here,
    in a key the wind, poor hint,
        can only do its best to emulate.

And yet these trees,
    despite the lift and loft,
        still hear some note of the tellurian:

every eucalyptus leaf hangs down,
    pointing backward, lured by gravity,
        dependent on a lower origin.

This delicate contrariety,
    an interplay of bearings
        the mind at once

can apprehend before it understands,
    gives each tree its philosophic look,
        as though the foliage were pondering,

like Seneca,[15] the state of things,
    the dark ancestral root
        holding tree and truth

firmly to the subterranean,
    and a million eucalyptus leaves
        called to another life, kindled

to rise again as perfume now
    in the hills all around,
        the smoke of eucalyptus

---

15 Seneca the Younger [4 BC–65 AD] was a Stoic Roman philosopher, statesman, and dramatist, primarily remembered for his tragedies, such as *Hercules Furens*, and for his letters on philosophy and ethics.

homesick for the supernatural
  and good, too, for keeping flies away,
    a method much used in these parts.

        2004

COST

I have an asset on my books that I
must carry and maintain despite the cost:
this body that I live in like a house,
a standalone for which I hold the deed.
Despite the cash invested, I have seen
nothing but diminishing returns.
The value goes in one direction, down,
and divest I cannot do. I'd like to find
a venture capitalist who'd look at me
with a klieg light of profit in his eyes,
or her eyes, but everyone's aware
that monies put here aren't recoverable.
My marketing budget swells with every year,
as what I have to advertise becomes
harder to find a market for. Demand
is correlated perfectly with time,
inversely so, as you might have guessed,
and the graph of the relationship is clear
in its predictability. At least
predictability is good, as those
whose job it is to manage risk will say.
They also advise we take into account
a worst-case scenario. Well, fine.
That's the only one I've got, as far
as I can see, so planning for it won't
be complicated, options will be few,
and returns on the investment I have made

won't keep my beneficiaries up
at night fighting over who gets what.
The thing I have will just depreciate,
the net effect of which will likely be
not foreclosure or eviction but
a rendering of my house unlivable,
an act of God that leaves me in the cold
zeroing out my balance in the books.

2021

TECHNE'S CLEARINGHOUSE

(George Washington Bridge, New York City)

Bridge out there in the big cold,
a bare location,
my storm-colored dominator

of ten million rivets
illumined in a nighttime
to which large things belong,

I want not just to speak to you,
but for you somehow to understand,
that I might make my way

a little less harrowingly
in the dispensation of things.
I've seen you on the long approach,

clean as a differential equation
strung between the Cloisters and the cliffs,
and I've fallen more than half in love

with planes of shifting light,
the diamonds in the traffic's lit-up veins,
and the voice of your megalomania:

like the sound of trains,
a deep angelus going out
to all the equipment we've devised,

the F-16, the dirty winch,
the cyclohexane refinery,
and your fair sister on the other side,

thrown and fury-fused,
who knows too well this litany.
I've been too long among these things,

too quiet, objectified like them,
using *thing* to indicate
whatever does its time

in Techne's clearinghouse,[16]
only now to find myself
inside among machinery

and fouled with distribution.
How far have we let it go,
the estrangement,

a bad marriage to utility
blinding us to higher purpose?
It's been too long,

this living, mute and paralyzed,
at the foot of buildings
as we've conceived them till now,

---

16 Techne, τέχνη in Greek, while originally denoting an art or craft, here suggests the merely
functional, as in the English "technique" or "technological."

the windy interchangeables.
My talking to you helps allay
the fear, always with me,

that you, the sad king of induration,
may be too far gone to understand.
Lording your geometry and lights,

you're everything I've always dreamed
the mineral kingdom could become.
What am I left with

when I need to speak of you,
an angle-iron deity
of arch, thrust, interval,

too big now for the name of *thing*,
an evacuated word. Yet if any
cleated spectacle can justify

that old capacious name, it's you,
Mammon's Harp, a system
for celebrating steel

while the bells ring out in pandemonium.
There is no end
to the trouble of things,

their gravity and fatigue.
Maybe I can help you in a way,
inured as I am, all my kind,

to wandering about, trying to make do
in a blizzard of phenomena.
Susceptible as I am

to every ghost of every chance,
I know that more inheres
than the trigonometric logic

you're so terribly welded to,
my real and glittering interlocutor.
Leaving, as I must,

the fixations of the engineer,
and risking reprisal
to listen in on what goes on

way up there in the cables
and towers in the wind,
I put these words to you.

2004

Dog

Is that the thing you found today,
the little gewgaw that you love?
It's a piece of Day-Glo rubber ball
you ardently dug out of the snow.
You are, my friend, a quadruped
that eats dirt and runs around.
I put my face among your paws,
where all good smells originate,
and stroke the velvet of your ear.
Inside, it smells like cumin seeds.
Are you the Other? Is that the game?
Well, I have two legs, you have four,
your breath is lovely, mine is foul,
and I speak French, while you do not,
and you eat sticks, though I do not,
and so if I were doctrinaire
(the word "dogmatic" I'll resist),
I'd say that we're as far apart
as Cain and Abel ever were

and that we didn't have much hope
of ever being cheek by jowl.
And yet we're *always* cheek to jowl!
You soak up love the way a weed
takes all it wants of water and light.
You keep your tchotchke close to you
and gather yourself to go to sleep
on the couch that's practically yours now.
You live an unexamined life,
but that's OK, you are a dog,
and who will cast the first stone?
Your brown, pulchritudinous eyes
drink me in, and I am yours
and hope that you can smell this love
I carry around, no questions asked,
for you, my dear digger, sleeping
like a dog beside me now.

2016

SORROW, MEISTER ECKHART SAID[17]

Sorrow, Meister Eckhart said,
comes of wanting what you cannot have,
and of wanting there is no end.
But what then does it mean

to say I want the world for you?
Not everything's available,
and of what is, there's much
you really would not want.

---

17 Meister Eckhart [1260–1328]: a German mystical theologian.

The burning jet fuel coming down
like rain does no one any good,
and the clear linear beauty
of rocket fire pouring down

upon some godforsaken hill
is death to some. And the grief
of *loving* what you cannot have,
a girl maybe, a way of life,

takes its sorry place in line
behind the horrors that arrive
inevitably like older boys
who've spent time in prison.

What I want doesn't seem
ever to have had a lot
to do with anything, but here
is what I want for you:

an educated, peaceful life
among the modest and the sane
but close enough to true toil
to know what it takes and takes away.

I'd like to fill your mind
with Eliot[18] and teach you to love
the feel of infield dirt,
and I don't want you to die,

but coffee in the cold dawn
is good, and you may be called upon
to fight, and sorrow has a way
of coming out to find you.

2016

---

18 T.S. Eliot [1888–1965]: an American poet and critic who was awarded the Nobel Prize in 1948.

Dana Gioia (1950)

Dana Gioia's impact on American culture has been formidable. The first poet to helm the National Endowment for the Arts, he has edited college textbooks and anthologies, written literary and cultural criticism, co-founded two major literary conferences, and worked to define the role of Catholic-American artists. In his 1991 *Atlantic Monthly* essay "Can Poetry Matter?" he called for a reinvigoration of American poetry by expanding it to incorporate the nearly lost skills of narrative, rhyme, and regular meter—a clarion call that caused an uproar. In the decades since, American poetry has steadily expanded to make more room for narrative and received forms.

As important as his role as public intellectual and literary critic has been, Gioia is first and foremost a poet, his work informed in equal part by sharp intelligence and deeply felt emotion. In addition to six poetry collections, he has written opera libretti, song cycles, and translations. In December 2015 he became the California State Poet Laureate.

Gioia was born in Hawthorne, California, an industrial suburb of Los Angeles, and grew up in a close-knit extended family of Mexican and Sicilian descent. The first member of his family to go to college, Gioia graduated from Stanford and then studied comparative literature at Harvard before returning to Stanford to earn an MBA. While working by day at General Foods, he wrote poetry by night. Fifteen years later he left his day job, moved with his family from New York to California's Sonoma Valley, and became one of the few contemporary poets to make a living as a full-time writer and public intellectual, co-editing college textbooks, writing critical essays for major newspapers, and contributing literary commentary to the British Broadcasting Company. During Gioia's chairmanship of the National Endowment for the Arts, he initiated popular programs such as The Big Read, Poetry Out Loud, and also Operation Homecoming, which provides writing workshops for US soldiers and their spouses. Gioia has taught at Colorado College, Johns Hopkins, Sarah Lawrence, Mercer, Wesleyan University, and, most recently, at the University of Southern California, where he was the Judge Widney Professor of Poetry and Public Culture. He quit his chair at USC in 2019 to resume his life as a full-time writer.

Selected Bibliography

Poems: *Daily Horoscope* (1986); *The Gods of Winter* (1991); *Interrogations at Noon* (2001); *Pity the Beautiful* (2012); *99 Poems: New & Selected* (2016); *Meet Me at the Lighthouse* (2023). Critical Collections: *Can Poetry Matter? Essays on Poetry and American Culture* (1992); *The Catholic Writer Today: And Other Essays* (2019). Memoir: *Studying with Miss Bishop: Memoirs from a Young Writer's Life* (2021).

THE NEXT POEM

How much better it seems now
than when it is finally done—
the unforgettable first line,
the cunning way the stanzas run.

The rhymes soft-spoken and suggestive
are barely audible at first,
an appetite not yet acknowledged
like the inkling of a thirst.

While gradually the form appears
as each line is coaxed aloud—
the architecture of a room
seen from the middle of a crowd.

The music that of common speech
but slanted so that each detail
sounds unexpected as a sharp
inserted in a simple scale.

No jumble box of imagery
dumped glumly in the reader's lap
or elegantly packaged junk
the unsuspecting must unwrap.

But words that could direct a friend
precisely to an unknown place,
those few unshakeable details
that no confusion can erase.

And the real subject left unspoken
but unmistakable to those
who don't expect a jungle parrot
in the black and white of prose.

How much better it seems now
than when it is finally written.
How hungrily one waits to feel
the bright lure seized, the old hook bitten.

1991

INTERROGATIONS AT NOON

Just before noon I often hear a voice,
Cool and insistent, whispering in my head.
It is the better man I might have been,
Who chronicles the life I've never led.

He cannot understand what grim mistake
Granted me life but left him still unborn.
He views his wayward brother with regret
And hardly bothers to disguise his scorn.

"Who is the person you pretend to be?"
He asks, "The failed saint, the simpering bore,
The pale connoisseur of spent desire,
The half-hearted hermit eyeing the door?

"You cultivate confusion like a rose
In watery lies too weak to be untrue,
And play the minor figures in the pageant,
Extravagant and empty, that is you."

2001

The Angel with the Broken Wing

I am the Angel with the Broken Wing,
The one large statue in this quiet room.
The staff finds me too fierce, and so they shut
Faith's ardor in this air-conditioned tomb.

The docents praise my elegant design
Above the chatter of the gallery.
Perhaps I am a masterpiece of sorts—
The perfect emblem of futility.

Mendoza carved me for a country church.
(His name's forgotten now except by me.)
I stood beside a gilded altar where
The hopeless offered God their misery.

I heard their women whispering at my feet—
Prayers for the lost, the dying, and the dead.
Their candles stretched my shadow up the wall,
And I became the hunger that they fed.

I broke my left wing in the Revolution
(Even a saint can savor irony)
When troops were sent to vandalize the chapel.
They hit me once—almost apologetically.

For even the godless feel something in a church,
A twinge of hope, fear? Who knows what it is?
A trembling unaccounted by their laws,
An ancient memory they can't dismiss.

There are so many things I must tell God!
The howling of the damned can't reach so high.
But I stand like a dead thing nailed to a perch,
A crippled saint against a painted sky.

2012

PENTECOST

After the death of our son

Neither the sorrows of afternoon, waiting in the silent house,
Nor the night no sleep relieves, when memory
Repeats its prosecution.

Nor the morning's ache for dream's illusion, nor any prayers
Improvised to an unknowable god
Can extinguish the flame.

We are not as we were. Death has been our pentecost,
And our innocence consumed by these implacable
Tongues of fire.

Comfort me with stones. Quench my thirst with sand.
I offer you this scarred and guilty hand
Until others mix our ashes.

2001

PLANTING A SEQUOIA

All afternoon my brothers and I have worked in the orchard,
Digging this hole, laying you into it, carefully packing the soil.
Rain blackened the horizon, but cold winds kept it over the Pacific,
And the sky above us stayed the dull gray
Of an old year coming to an end.

In Sicily a father plants a tree to celebrate his first son's birth—
An olive or a fig tree—a sign that the earth has one more life to bear.
I would have done the same, proudly laying new stock into my father's orchard,
A green sapling rising among the twisted apple boughs,
A promise of new fruit in other autumns.

But today we kneel in the cold planting you, our native giant,
Defying the practical custom of our fathers,
Wrapping in your roots a lock of hair, a piece of an infant's birth cord,
All that remains above earth of a first-born son,
A few stray atoms brought back to the elements.

We will give you what we can—our labor and our soil,
Water drawn from the earth when the skies fail,
Nights scented with the ocean fog, days softened by the circuit of bees.
We plant you in the corner of the grove, bathed in western light,
A slender shoot against the sunset.

And when our family is no more, all of his unborn brothers dead,
Every niece and nephew scattered, the house torn down,
His mother's beauty ashes in the air,
I want you to stand among strangers, all young and ephemeral to you,
Silently keeping the secret of your birth.

1991

COUNTING THE CHILDREN

I.

"This must have been her bedroom, Mr. Choi.
It's hard to tell. The only other time
I came back here was when I found her body."

Neither of us belonged there. She lived next door.
I was the accountant sent out by the State
To take an inventory of the house.

When someone wealthy dies without a will,
The court sends me to audit the estate.
They know that strangers trust a man who listens.

The neighbor led me down an unlit hall.
We came up to a double door and stopped.
She whispered as if someone else were near.

"She used to wander around town at night
And rifle through the trash. We all knew that.
But what we didn't know about was *them*."

She stepped inside and fumbled for a switch.
It didn't work, but light leaked through the curtains.
"Come in," she said. "I want to show you hell."

I walked into a room of wooden shelves
Stretching from floor to ceiling, wall to wall,
With smaller shelves arranged along the center.

A crowd of faces looked up silently.
Shoulder to shoulder, standing all in rows,
Hundreds of dolls were lining every wall.

Not a collection anyone would want—
Just ordinary dolls salvaged from the trash
With dozens of each kind all set together.

Some battered, others missing arms and legs,
Shelf after shelf of the same dusty stare
As if despair could be assuaged by order.

They looked like sisters huddling in the dark,
Forgotten brides abandoned at the altar,
Their veils turned yellow, dresses stiff and soiled.

Rows of discarded little girls and babies—
Some naked, others dressed for play—they wore
Whatever lives their owners left them in.

Where were the children who promised them love?
The small, caressing hands, the lips which whispered
Secrets in the dark? Once they were woken,

Each by name. Now they have become each other—
Anonymous except for injury,
The beautiful and headless side by side.

Was this where all lost childhoods go? These dim
Abandoned rooms, these crude arrangements staged
For settled dust and shadow, left to prove

That all affection is outgrown, or show
The uniformity of our desire?
How dismal someone else's joy can be.

I stood between the speechless shelves and knew
Dust has a million lives, the heart has one.
I turned away and started my report.

II.

That night I dreamt of working on a ledger,
A book so large it stretched across my desk,
Thousands of numbers running down each page.

I knew I had to settle the account,
Yet as I tried to calculate the total,
The numbers started slipping down the page,

Suddenly breaking up like Scrabble letters
Brushed into a box to end a game,
Each strained-for word uncoupled back to nil.

But as I tried to add them back together
And hold each number on the thin green line
Where it belonged, I realized that now

Nothing I did would ever fit together.
In my hands even 2 + 2 + 2
No longer equaled anything at all.

And then I saw my father there beside me.
He asked me why I couldn't find the sum.
He held my daughter crying in his arms.

My family stood behind him in a row,
Uncles and aunts, cousins I'd never seen,
My grandparents from China and their parents,

All of my family, living and dead,
A line that stretched as far as I could see.
Even the strangers called to me by name.

And now I saw I wasn't at my desk
But working on the coffin of my daughter,
And she would die unless I found the sum.

But I had lost too many of the numbers.
They tumbled to the floor and blazed on fire.
I saw the dolls then—screaming in the flames.

III.

When I awoke, I sat up straight in bed.
The sweaty sheet was twisted in my hands.
My heart was pounding. Had I really screamed?

But no, my wife was still asleep beside me.
I got up quietly and found my robe,
Knowing I couldn't fall asleep again.

Then groping down the unlit hall, I saw
A soft-edged light beneath my daughter's door.
It was the night-light plugged in by her bed.

And I remembered when she was a baby,
How often I would get up in the night
And creep into that room to watch her sleep.

I never told my wife how many times
I came to check each night—or that I was
Always afraid of what I might discover.

I felt so helpless standing by her crib,
Watching the quiet motions of her breath
In the half-darkness of the faint night-light.

How delicate this vessel in our care,
This gentle soul we summoned to the world,
A life we treasured but could not protect.

This was the terror I could not confess—
Not even to my wife—and it was the joy
My daughter had no words to understand.

So standing at my pointless watch each night
In the bare nursery we had improvised,
I learned the loneliness that we call love.

IV.

But I gave up those vigils years ago.
My daughter's seven now, and I don't worry—
At least no more than any father does.

But waking up last night after the dream,
Trembling in the hall, looking at her door,
I let myself be drawn into her room.

She was asleep—the blankets softly rising
And falling with each breath, the faint light tracing
The sleek unfoldings of her long black hair.

Then suddenly I felt myself go numb.
And though you won't believe that an accountant
Can have a vision, I will tell you mine.

Each of us thinks our own child beautiful,
But watching her and marveling at the sheer
Smoothness of skin without a scar or blemish,

I saw beyond my daughter to all children,
And though elated, still I felt confused
Because I wondered why I never sensed

That thrill of joy when looking at adults
No matter how refined or beautiful,
Why lust or envy always intervened.

There is no *tabula rasa* for the soul.
Each spirit, be it infant, bird or flower,
Comes to the world perfected and complete,

And only time proves its unraveling.
But I'm digressing from my point, my vision.
What I meant to say is merely this:

What if completion comes only in beginnings?
The naked tree exploding into flower?
And all our prim assumptions about time

Prove wrong? What if we cannot read the future
Because our destiny moves back in time,
And only memory speaks prophetically?

We long for immortality, a soul
To rise up flaming from the body's dust.
I know that it exists. I felt it there,

Perfect and eternal in the way
That only numbers are, intangible but real,
Infinitely divisible yet whole.

But we do not possess it in ourselves.
We die, and it abides, and we are one
With all our ancestors, while it divides

Over and over, common to us all,
The ancient face returning in the child,
The distant arms embracing us, the salt

Of our blind origins filling our veins.
I stood confused beside my daughter's bed
Surprised to find the room around me dim.

Then glancing at the bookshelf in the corner,
I saw she'd lined her dolls up in a row.
Three little girls were sitting in the dark.

Their sharp glass eyes surveyed me with contempt.
They recognized me only as a rival,
The one whose world would keep no place for them.

I felt like holding them tight in my arms,
Promising I would never let them go,
But they would trust no promises of mine.

I feared that if I touched one, it would scream.

1991

Summer Storm

We stood on the rented patio
While the party went on inside.
You knew the groom from college.
I was a friend of the bride.

We hugged the brownstone wall behind us
To keep our dress clothes dry
And watched the sudden summer storm
Floodlit against the sky.

The rain was like a waterfall
Of brilliant beaded light,
Cool and silent as the stars
The storm hid from the night.

To my surprise you took my arm—
A gesture you didn't explain—
And we spoke in whispers, as if we two
Might imitate the rain.

Then suddenly the storm receded
As swiftly as it came.
The doors behind us opened up.
The hostess called your name.

I watched you merge into the group,
Aloof and yet polite.
We didn't speak another word
Except to say good-night.

Why does that evening's memory
Return with this night's storm—
A party twenty years ago,
Its disappointments warm?

There are so many *might-have-beens*,
What-ifs that won't stay buried,
Other cities, other jobs,
Strangers we might have married.

And memory insists on pining
For places it never went,
As if life would be happier
Just by being different.

2001

MARRIAGE OF MANY YEARS

Most of what happens happens beyond words.
The lexicon of lip and fingertip
defies translation into common speech.
I recognize the musk of your dark hair.
It always thrills me, though I can't describe it.
My finger on your thigh does not touch skin—
it touches *your* skin warming to my touch.
You are a language I have learned by heart.

This intimate patois will vanish with us,
its only native speakers. Does it matter?
Our tribal chants, our dances round the fire
performed the sorcery we most required.
They bound us in a spell time could not break.
Let the young vaunt their ecstasy. We keep
our tribe of two in sovereign secrecy.
What must be lost was never lost on us.

2016

Marie Howe (1950)

Born in Rochester, New York, Marie Howe was the oldest girl in a family of nine children. She attended Sacred Heart Convent School and the University of Windsor. After graduating, she worked as a reporter for a Rochester newspaper and taught high school English near Boston. At age thirty, Howe took a summer class in poetry, an experience about which she has said, "Every once in a while, we walk through a door and we realize, 'My God, it's the right door. This is the door I was meant to walk through.'" Howe went on to devote herself to poetry, earning an MFA from Columbia University.

In 1987 Margaret Atwood chose Howe's debut collection, *The Good Thief,* for the National Poetry Series. The book went on to receive a Lavan Younger Poets Award from the Academy of American Poets. Judge Stanley Kunitz wrote, "Her long, deep-breathing lines address the mysteries of flesh and spirit, in terms accessible only to a woman who is very much of our time and yet still in touch with the sacred." *What the Living Do*, Howe's follow-up collection, centers on poems about her family, particularly her brother, John, who died in 1989 of an AIDS-related illness. With Michael Klein, Howe also co-edited an anthology of essays, *In the Company of My Solitude: American Writers from the AIDS Pandemic.* Each of Howe's four luminous poetry collections explores Catholic spirituality and depicts, in her own words, "the spiritual dimensions of life as they present themselves in this world."

Howe has been awarded fellowships from the Bunting Institute at Radcliffe College, the National Endowment for the Arts, the Guggenheim Foundation, and the Fine Arts Work Center in Provincetown. She has taught at Columbia University, Tufts University, Warren Wilson College, Dartmouth College, New York University, and Sarah Lawrence College. In 2018 she was elected a Chancellor of the Academy of American Poets. Poet Laureate of New York State from 2012–2014, she lives in New York City with her daughter.

Selected Bibliography

Poems: *The Good Thief* (1988); *What the Living Do* (1998); *The Kingdom of Ordinary Time* (2008); *Magdalene* (2017); *New and Selected Poems* (2024). As co-editor, with Michael Klein, *In the Company of My Solitude: American Writing from the AIDS Pandemic* (1995).

THE STAR MARKET

The people Jesus loved were shopping at The Star Market yesterday.
An old lead-colored man standing next to me at the checkout
breathed so heavily I had to step back a few steps.

Even after his bags were packed he still stood, breathing hard and
hawking into his hand. The feeble, the lame, I could hardly look at them:
shuffling through the aisles, they smelled of decay, as if The Star Market

had declared a day off for the able-bodied, and I had wandered in
with the rest of them: sour milk, bad meat:
looking for cereal and spring water.

Jesus must have been a saint, I said to myself, looking for my lost car
in the parking lot later, stumbling among the people who would have
been lowered into rooms by ropes, who would have crept

out of caves or crawled from the corners of public baths on their hands
and knees begging for mercy.

If I touch only the hem of his garment, one woman thought,
could I bear the look on his face when he wheels around?

2008

THE SNOW STORM

I walked down towards the river, and the deer had left tracks
deep as half my arm, that ended in a perfect hoof
and the shump shump sound my boots made walking made the silence loud.

And when I turned back towards the great house
I walked beside the deer tracks again.
And when I came near the feeder: little tracks of the birds on the surface
     of the snow I'd broken through.

Put your finger here, and see my hands, then bring your hand and put it in my side.

I put my hand down into the deer track
     and touched the bottom of an invisible hoof.
Then my finger in the little mark of the jay.

            2008

The Boy

My older brother is walking down the sidewalk into the suburban summer
 night:
white T-shirt, blue jeans—to the field at the end of the street.

Hangers Hideout the boys called it, an undeveloped plot, a pit overgrown
with weeds, some old furniture thrown down there,

and some metal hangers clinking in the trees like wind chimes.
He's running away from home because our father wants to cut his hair.

And in two more days our father will convince me to go to him—you know
where he is—and talk to him: No reprisals. He promised. A small parade of
 kids

in feet pajamas will accompany me, their voices like the first peepers in spring.
And my brother will walk ahead of us home, and my father

will shave his head bald, and my brother will not speak to anyone the next
month, not a word, not *pass the milk*, nothing.

What happened in our house taught my brothers how to leave, how to walk
down a sidewalk without looking back.

I was the girl. What happened taught me to follow him, whoever he was,
calling and calling his name.

1998

WHAT THE LIVING DO

Johnny, the kitchen sink has been clogged for days, some utensil probably fell
    down there.
And the Drano won't work but smells dangerous, and the crusty dishes have
    piled up

waiting for the plumber I still haven't called. This is the everyday we spoke of.
It's winter again: the sky's a deep, headstrong blue, and the sunlight pours
    through

the open living room windows because the heat's on too high in here, and I
      can't turn it off.
For weeks now, driving, or dropping a bag of groceries in the street, the bag
      breaking,

I've been thinking: This is what the living do. And yesterday, hurrying along
    those
wobbly bricks in the Cambridge sidewalk, spilling my coffee down my wrist
    and sleeve,

I thought it again, and again later, when buying a hairbrush: This is it.
Parking. Slamming the car door shut in the cold. What you called *that*
    yearning.

What you finally gave up. We want the spring to come and the winter to pass.
    We want

whoever to call or not call, a letter, a kiss—we want more and more and then
     more of it.

But there are moments, walking, when I catch a glimpse of myself in the
    window glass,
say, the window of the corner video store, and I'm gripped by a cherishing so
    deep

for my own blowing hair, chapped face, and unbuttoned coat that I'm
    speechless:
I am living. I remember you.

                               1998

My Mother's Body

Bless my mother's body, the first song of her beating
heart and her breathing, her voice, which I could dimly hear,

grew louder. From inside her body I heard almost every word she said.
Within that girl I drove to the store and back, her feet pressing

the pedals of the blue car, her voice, first gate to the cold sunny mornings,
rain, moonlight, snow fall, dogs...

Her kidneys failed, the womb where I once lived is gone.
Her young astonished body pushed me down that long corridor,

and my body hurt her, I know that—24 years old. I'm old enough
to be that girl's mother, to smooth her hair, to look into her exultant
    frightened eyes,

her bedsheets stained with chocolate, her heart in constant failure.
It's a girl, someone must have said. She must have kissed me

with her mouth, first grief, first air,
and soon I was drinking her, first food, I was eating my mother,

slumped in her wheelchair, one of my brothers pushing it
across the snowy lawn, her eyes fixed, her face averted.

Bless this body she made, my long legs, her long arms and fingers,
our voice in my throat speaking to you now.

2008

What We Would Give Up

One morning in Orlando Florida, I asked a group of college students—
What would we be willing to give up to equalize the wealth in the world?
Malls, a red-haired young woman said right away. Supermarkets, the young
man in a black T-shirt said—where you go to buy bread, and there's a
hundred and fifty loaves on the shelf. Imported fruit, the young woman
sitting next to him said—berries in winter. A car, the guy with the nose ring
said, I don't have a car anyway.

Travel? Jet fuel? Well, we'd all be together, someone said. TV, said the guy
without a car, I don't watch TV anyway. What about coffee, I said, looking
down at my double tall half-caf soy latte. Ok, everyone said, but I wondered
about that one. Ten pairs of shoes? Yes. Movies? Maybe.

That week my phone was out of order. When the company tried to connect
my line to a split line that would allow me fast cable access to the Internet
everything went dead. When I called the phone company I was put on hold
and had to listen to a tinny version of Vivaldi's *Four Seasons* pitched at what
seemed a much faster than usual speed. *This call may be monitored.*

I was told to punch my number in five times during that first phone call, and
every time I was transferred to a person who asked for my number again.

Eight calls that first day. We'll send a technician out, the central office would say. The technician, when he arrived would say, The problem is in the central office. When I called the central office, someone would say, We have to send a technician out. When I said, a technician has already been there, the central office person would say, All I can do is put in an order Ma'am. Vivaldi.

After seven days, I began to suspect that at the center of the central office is a room empty of all furniture but a table. On the table, a ringing telephone. Somewhere way down a long corridor, one guy in a broken chair in front of an empty desk. Every once in a while he cranes his neck towards the door and yells to no one in particular—is anyone gonna answer that?

If you don't want music, the phone company says, please hold through the silence.

When I came home from Orlando, the phone started working again. The Gap? Someone said. Everybody said, I don't go to The Gap.

Would I give up the telephone? Would I give up hot water? Would I give up makeup? Would I give up dyeing my hair? That was a hard one. If I stopped dyeing my hair everyone would know that my golden hair is actually gray, and my long American youth would be over—and then what?

2008

EASTER

Two of the fingers on his right hand
had been broken

so when he poured back into that hand it surprised
him—it hurt him at first.

And the whole body was too small. Imagine
the sky trying to fit into a tunnel carved into a hill.

He came into it two ways:
From the outside, as we step into a pair of pants.

And from the center—suddenly all at once.
Then he felt himself awake in the dark alone.

2008

PRAYER

Every day I want to speak with you. And every day something more
    important
calls for my attention—the drugstore, the beauty products, the luggage

I need to buy for the trip.
Even now I can hardly sit here

among the falling piles of paper and clothing, the garbage trucks outside
already screeching and banging.

The mystics say you are as close as my own breath.
Why do I flee from you?

My days and nights pour through me like complaints
and become a story I forgot to tell.

Help me. Even as I write these words I am planning
to rise from the chair as soon as I finish this sentence.

2008

Brigit Pegeen Kelly (1951–2016)

Because Brigit Pegeen Kelly was an intensely private person, little is known about her life. Born in Palo Alto, California, she grew up in Southern Indiana. A beloved and influential instructor, she taught at various colleges and universities, including the University of California-Irvine, Purdue University, Warren Wilson College, and, for much of her career, at the University of Illinois in Urbana-Champaign. A former student has written of Kelly, "She was not one for showy demonstration of emotion. But her love—and that is what it is, in the end, what every dedicated teacher gives her students—was as enormous, complex, and humble as a prairie."

Kelly is widely admired for the originality and craftsmanship of her poems, which poet Carl Phillips has said are "like no one else's—hard and luminous, weird in the sense of making a thing strange, that we at last might see it, poems that from book to book show a strength that flexes itself both formally and in terms of content, in ways that continue to, at equal turns, teach and surprise." Kelly's first collection, *To the Place of Trumpets*, was chosen by James Merrill for the Yale Series of Younger Poets. In his foreword, Merrill praised how Kelly's work transmutes her Catholic upbringing "beyond any taint of dogma." Kelly's second collection received the prestigious Lamont Poetry Prize of the Academy of American Poets, and she went on to receive many other honors, including a Discovery/*The Nation* Award, a Whiting Writers Award, and fellowships from the Guggenheim Foundation and the National Endowment for the Arts. The journals that published her poems include *The Antioch Review*, *New England Review*, *The Kenyon Review*, *Third Coast*, and *Prairie Schooner*.

Selected Bibliography
To the Place of Trumpets (1988); *Song* (1995); *The Orchard* (2004).

PETITION

These are the long weeks. The weeks
Of waiting. Let them be
Longer. Let the days smolder
Like the peat slung
In plastic sacks by the greenhouse
And let the seedlings not rush
Into growth but climb the air slowly
As if it were a ladder,
One small foot at a time.
Let the fetid smell of bone meal
Be the body unlocking
As the river does, slowing to a hazy laze
That pulls the boaters in
And makes the fish rise up. And
As the wide-wheeled yellow tractors
Roll along the highway,
Stalling traffic in their wakes,
And the dust from the playing fields
Settles over us like pollen,
Like the balls dropping softly
Into our mitts, let
The willow's love of water—
Its dark and beaded rain—
Be the only storm we long for.

1995

THE VISITATION

God sends his tasks
and one does
them or not, but the sky
delivers its gifts
at the appointed
times: With spit and sigh,
with that improbable
burst of flame, the balloon
comes over
the cornfield, bringing
another country
with it, bringing
from a long way off
those colors that are at first
the low sound
of a horn, but soon
are many horns, and clocks,
and bells, and clappers
and your heart
rising to the silence
in all of them, a silence
so complete that
the heads of the corn
bow back before it
and the dog flees in terror
down the road
and you alone are left
gazing up
at three solemn visitors
swinging
in a golden cage
beneath that unbelievable chorus of red
and white, swinging
so close you cannot move
or speak, so close

the road grows wet with light,
as when the sun flares
after an evening storm
and you become weightless, falling
back in the air
before the giant oak
that with a fiery burst
the balloon
just clears.

1988

THE GARDEN OF THE TRUMPET TREE

Someone stuck an apple in the stone head's open mouth. A grave insult. But I did not take it out. Maybe a boy did it, running through the gardens at night, his pockets full of fruit. Or maybe it was a ghost bored with its lot. It does not matter. Today I stood for the first time before the bodiless head and the strange flowering tree it guards. I tried not to laugh. The head on its post stood no taller than I. The head that had bullied me for so long, the great stone head that only the darkness had been able to silence, bagging it each night with a soft cloth sack, the way the heads of those to be hanged are bagged, made no sound. I tried not to think: This is your just desert: Pillar of pride, pilloried. I touched with both hands the eyes of the head the way a blind person might. They were huge and swollen like the eyes of the deaf composer, or the eyes of the mad poet who left his wife alone while he spent his days in paradise. I touched with one finger the warm fruit. Against the pale cast of the stone the apple shone uncommonly bright, and behind it the thousand and thousand blossoms of the trumpet tree shone uncommonly bright. The fruit and the blossoms were the same scarlet color, and I could see for the first time in the yellow morning light the curious tree for what it was. Not a tree in flower, as I had so long thought, but a flowerless tree coupled with a blossoming trumpet vine. The vine had grown snakelike up and around the trunk, and it had grown so large it had half-strangled the small tree, crawling over every branch and shoot, until the vine and the tree were almost indistinguishable, green flesh and charred wood, flowers and rot, a new creation, a trumpet tree, tree out of time, the smoldering center of some medieval dream. The flowers swam forward in the light, each scarlet bloom so intricate and unlikely—downswung, fluted, narrower than the narrowest piping, forked with yellow silk—it looked as if it had been sewn by hand, the whole improbable tree looked as if it had been worked with impossible patience by a woman's pale hands. Bees stumbled in and out, shaking the flowers. From nowhere a hummingbird appeared, iridescent, green, flipping its shining tail, a creature more fish than bird, more insect than fish, spinning and sipping. To nowhere it returned. The garden stood perfectly still. And for a moment in that garden it seemed as if sound and silence were the same thing, for a moment it seemed as if the thousand and thousand tiny trumpets were blowing a thousand and thousand shining notes, blown glass notes, the liquid substance of the air itself, glass and fire, the morning flushed to perfect fullness. I stood for a long time, breathing in the strange perfume of those scentless flowers. I thought of how the crow would come in an hour or two and plant his dusty feet on the carved head and pluck the fruit apart, piece by sweetened piece. I looked at the blossoming tree. I looked at the stone head. I touched the warm fruit. And I took the apple out. There was no sound. It was like closing the eyes of the dead.

2004

Song

Listen: there was a goat's head hanging by ropes in a tree.
All night it hung there and sang. And those who heard it
Felt a hurt in their hearts and thought they were hearing
The song of a night bird. They sat up in their beds, and then
They lay back down again. In the night wind, the goat's head
Swayed back and forth, and from far off it shone faintly
The way the moonlight shone on the train track miles away
Beside which the goat's headless body lay. Some boys
Had hacked its head off. It was harder work than they had imagined.
The goat cried like a man and struggled hard. But they

Finished the job. They hung the bleeding head by the school
And then ran off into the darkness that seems to hide everything.
The head hung in the tree. The body lay by the tracks.
The head called to the body. The body to the head.
They missed each other. The missing grew large between them,
Until it pulled the heart right out of the body, until
The drawn heart flew toward the head, flew as a bird flies
Back to its cage and the familiar perch from which it trills.
Then the heart sang in the head, softly at first and then louder,
Sang long and low until the morning light came up over
The school and over the tree, and then the singing stopped....
The goat had belonged to a small girl. She named
The goat Broken Thorn Sweet Blackberry, named it after
The night's bush of stars, because the goat's silky hair
Was dark as well water, because it had eyes like wild fruit.
The girl lived near a high railroad track. At night
She heard the trains passing, the sweet sound of the train's horn
Pouring softly over her bed, and each morning she woke
To give the bleating goat his pail of warm milk. She sang
Him songs about girls with ropes and cooks in boats.
She brushed him with a stiff brush. She dreamed daily
That he grew bigger, and he did. She thought her dreaming
Made it so. But one night the girl didn't hear the train's horn,
And the next morning she woke to an empty yard. The goat
Was gone. Everything looked strange. It was as if a storm
Had passed through while she slept, wind and stones, rain
Stripping the branches of fruit. She knew that someone
Had stolen the goat and that he had come to harm. She called
To him. All morning and into the afternoon, she called
And called. She walked and walked. In her chest a bad feeling
Like the feeling of the stones gouging the soft undersides
Of her bare feet. Then somebody found the goat's body
By the high tracks, the flies already filling their soft bottles
At the goat's torn neck. Then somebody found the head
Hanging in a tree by the school. They hurried to take
These things away so that the girl would not see them.
They hurried to raise money to buy the girl another goat.
They hurried to find the boys who had done this, to hear

Them say it was a joke, a joke, it was nothing but a joke....
But listen: here is the point. The boys thought to have
Their fun and be done with it. It was harder work than they
Had imagined, this silly sacrifice, but they finished the job,
Whistling as they washed their large hands in the dark.
What they didn't know was that the goat's head was already
Singing behind them in the tree. What they didn't know
Was that the goat's head would go on singing, just for them,
Long after the ropes were down, and that they would learn to listen,
Pail after pail, stroke after patient stroke. They would
Wake in the night thinking they heard the wind in the trees
Or a night bird, but their hearts beating harder. There
Would be a whistle, a hum, a high murmur, and, at last, a song,
The low song a lost boy sings remembering his mother's call.
Not a cruel song, no, no, not cruel at all. This song
Is sweet. It is sweet. The heart dies of this sweetness.

1995

The Satyr's Heart

Now I rest my head on the satyr's carved chest,
The hollow where the heart would have been, if sandstone
Had a heart, if a headless goat man could have a heart.
His neck rises to a dull point, points upward
To something long gone, elusive, and at his feet
The small flowers swarm, earnest and sweet, a clamor
Of white, a clamor of blue, and black the sweating soil
They breed in....If I sit without moving, how quickly
Things change, birds turning tricks in the trees,
Colorless birds and those with color, the wind fingering
The twigs, and the furred creatures doing whatever
Furred creatures do. So, and so. There is the smell of fruit
And the smell of wet coins. There is the sound of a bird
Crying, and the sound of water that does not move....

If I pick the dead iris? If I wave it above me
Like a flag, a blazoned flag? My fanfare? Little fare
With which I buy my way, making things brave?
No, that is not it. Uncovering what is brave. The way
Now I bend over and with my foot turn up a stone,
And there they are: the armies of pale creatures who
Without cease or doubt sew the sweet sad earth.

2004

April Lindner (1962)

April Lindner was raised in the suburbs near Long Island's south shore. When she was in her early teens, the family moved to New Hampshire, and she graduated from the University of New Hampshire, where she studied under the poets Charles Simic and Mekeel McBride. After graduation, Lindner worked as an Editor for Clinical Affairs at Boston University Medical Center before moving back to New York, where she earned an MFA from Sarah Lawrence College. After completing this degree, Lindner worked as an Editorial Assistant at Cambridge University Press, taught English at The Ursuline School in New Rochelle, and spent time as a stay-at-home mother. In 1998 she graduated with a PhD in English from the University of Cincinnati.

Lindner is the author of two collections of poetry. *Skin* (2002) won the prestigious Walt McDonald First Book Prize, and *This Bed Our Bodies Shaped* (2012) was runner-up for the Able Muse Book Prize. Her poems, described by Denise Duhamel as "tender and fierce, startling in their excavations," frequently address the submerged tensions and joys of domestic life. Subtle in both its vision and its musicality, her poetry explores childhood, erotic desire, motherhood, and religious experience with equal aplomb. Quietly epiphanic, Lindner's best poems offer, as Thomas Lux writes, "collisions between vulnerability and unflinching looks at our human condition, its truths and contradictions." Lindner also writes young adult fiction. Her three young adult novels—*Jane*, *Catherine*, and *Love, Lucy*—are retellings of classic British novels, *Jane Eyre*, *Wuthering Heights*, and *A Room with a View*, respectively. She has edited and co-edited several poetry anthologies, including *Contemporary American Poetry*, co-edited with R. S. Gwynn, and *Líneas conectadas*, a bilingual anthology of contemporary American poets translated into Spanish for a Mexican audience.

Currently, Lindner is a professor at Saint Joseph's University, Philadelphia's Jesuit university. On a school-sponsored Ignatian Pilgrimage to Northern Spain and Rome, Lindner was moved to return to the Catholic faith of her early childhood, and subsequently enrolled in an RCIA program, getting confirmed at age 48. The mother of two adult sons, Lindner lives in Stockton, New Jersey, with her husband and three rescue dogs.

Selected Bibliography
Poems: *Skin* (2002); *This Bed Our Bodies Shaped* (2012). Young Adult Novels: *Jane* (2010); *Catherine* (2014); *Love, Lucy* (2016). Literary monographs: *Marilyn Nelson* (2011); *New Formalist Poetry of the American West* (2001).

LEARNING TO FLOAT

Relax. It's like love. Keep your lips
moist and parted, let your upturned hands
unfold like water lilies, palms exposed.

Breathe deeply, slowly. Forget chlorine
and how the cement bottom was stained
blue so the water looks clear

and Caribbean. Ignore the drowned mosquitoes,
the twigs that gather in the net
of your hair. The sun is your ticket,

your narcotic, blessing your chin,
the floating islands of your knees.
Shut your eyes and give yourself

to the pulsating starfish, purple and red,
that flicker on your inner lids.
Hallucination is part of the process,

like amnesia. Forget how you learned
to swim, forget being told
Don't panic. Don't worry. Let go

of my neck. It's only water. Don't think
unless you're picturing Chagall,
his watercolors of doves and rooftops,

lovers weightless as tissue,
gravity banished, the dissolving voices
of violins and panpipes. The man's hand

circles the woman's wrist so loosely,
what moors her permits her to float,
and she rises past the water's skin,

above verandas and the tossing heads
of willows. Her one link to earth,
his light—almost reluctant—touch, is a rope

unfurling, slipping her past the horizon,
into the cloud-stirring current. This far up,
What can she do but trust he won't let go?

2002

St. Theresa in Ecstasy

after Gian Lorenzo Bernini

The angel, when he comes at last
in a trumpet blast of light
glistens like a newborn, smooth
of cheek and chest, his slender waist
cinched in wind-washed gauze. She'd willed
this visit, prayed for days, refusing
sleep and food. Now he appears
beside her, naked arm drawn back.
His fingertips caress a spear,
point it at her heart; his smile
betrays amusement. This could be
the moment just before his arrow
plunges through her breast—*as if
to pierce my very entrails,*
she would write—or it could be
the aftermath. Her heavy vestments
lift and rustle; from their depths
she swoons, lips parted, body curling
upward toward that flame-tipped arrow,
that cauterizing point, and though
the whole tableau is stone, she vibrates
like a harp string as the hand
draws back. One bare foot clings to earth

as, limp, she crests a wave of pain
surpassing sweetness, tasted once
and hungered after: *Now the soul
is satisfied with nothing less.*

2012

Our Lady of Perpetual Help

The burnt church up the street yawns to the sky,
its empty windows edged in soot, its portals
boarded up and slathered with graffiti,
oily layers, urgent but illegible.
All that can be plundered has been, all
but the carapace—the hollow bell tower,
the fieldstone box that once served as a nave.
The tidy row of homes that line this block
have tended lawns and scalloped bathtub shrines.
Each front porch holds a chair where no one sits.
Those who live here triple lock their doors
day and night. Some mornings they step out
to find a smoking car stripped to its skeleton
abandoned at the curb. Most afternoons
the street is still but for a mourning dove
and gangs of pigeons picking through the grass.
Our Lady of Perpetual Help is gray,
a dead incisor in a wary smile.
A crevice in her wall allows a glimpse
into the chancel, where a sodden mattress
and dirty blanket indicate that someone
finds this place a sanctuary still,
takes his rest here, held and held apart
from passersby, their cruelties and their kindnesses,
watched over by the night's blind congregation,
by the blank eyes of a concrete saint.

2012

FONTANEL

Here's the ravine, a stretch of skin
spanning the breach like a footbridge.
Canvas-thin, it trembles with the blood
that runs beneath. Something less tangible
courses there too, a whitewater flume
of images: the stretching housecat;
car keys that sing and catch light;
floorboards knotted with dark, animal eyes;
the window with its shifting square of sky.
All things equal, each thing startling,
And everything unmediated by the mind's
habitual grapple with *why*
and *so what*. You frown at a faded
wallpaper pineapple, and the membrane
flutters harder. I'm careful
when I comb your sparse brown hair.
When I sing your name I borrow a lilt
I'd never use in speech. The words
don't matter; I'm saying drink me while you can,
like milk. Let me be flesh and flannel,
hands that loosen your tangled blanket.
Know me by scent before you learn my name,
before doorknobs turn into doorknobs,
before the gates knit shut.

2002

CARRIED AWAY

One rainy night we sat in traffic
and, overtired in back, you saw
a wind-whipped grocery bag afloat
beyond the clutch of jagged branches,
swept by gusts and whirled in eddies.
A sudden downdraft swooped it earthward,
where it danced till with a whoosh
a current luffed it past the powerlines.
Disowned by gravity, small ghost
not yet snagged by twiggy fingers,
it couldn't reach the earth. Thin-skinned,
it pulsed, translucent jellyfish.
You wept and pled to be let out
into the dark and slanted rain,
to somehow save that desolate thing.
The light turned green and still you begged,
Go back, go back, on its behalf,
caught and held, bossed and tossed
by a will much greater than its own.

2012

THE TRIP TO BROOKLYN MISREMEMBERED AS A ROLLER COASTER RIDE

Lock your doors, they'd say. *Look straight ahead.*
Every other Saturday we'd travel
from Long Island to Grandma's house in Brooklyn,
my parents anxiously accelerating
through neighborhoods they'd gladly left behind.
In the backseat, secretly, we thrilled
with vertigo, craning our necks to gape

at tenements and billboards. We admired
the smashed-out windows and oily graffiti—
so much more satisfying than the misdeeds
we dared dream up. Buckled in the backseat,
we drowsed, secure. But once Dad took a wrong turn
past a cemetery—not the first I'd seen,
but enormous: rows and rows of headstones
in strict formation, interspersed by obelisks
and mausoleums dreadful in their heaviness.
A graveyard gray and scalloped as the ocean
and seemingly as endless, stretching on
for blocks until I couldn't help but know:
the dead were gaining on the living, soon
they would be everywhere. I squinched my eyes
and counted ten but when I peeked we still
were driving past tombstones that grew more ancient,
pale and straight at first, but later crooked,
dark with car exhaust, ground down by age—
the way our grandmother kept growing shorter—
the city underground crowded with bodies
like the one above, each skeleton
waiting in its windowless apartment,
and everyone I'd ever grow to love
would wind up buried here. Our Buick climbed
the ramp onto the Brooklyn-Queens Expressway,
a clackety, steep track. Chains scraped us onward,
grinding toward a peak high as a skyscraper—
a long pause—then the sudden giddy plunge,
the Naugahyde seats falling out beneath us.
We hovered, breathless, bracing for the drop.

2012

Orlando Ricardo Menes (1958)

Orlando Ricardo Menes was born to Cuban parents in Lima, Perú. Forced by a *coup d'état* to flee Perú when Menes was ten years old, his family immigrated to the United States, where they lived in the Miami area. In the early 1970s, Menes lived for two years in Francoist Spain before returning to the US, where he earned both a BA and an MA from the University of Florida and, subsequently, a PhD from the University of Illinois-Chicago. Since 2000, Menes has been a professor of English at the University of Notre Dame, and he is currently the poetry editor of the *Notre Dame Review*. In addition to original collections of verse, Menes has edited two anthologies, including *Renaming Ecstasy: Latino Writings on the Sacred* (Bilingual Press, 2004), and he has published *My Heart Flooded with Water* (Latin American Literary Review Press, 2009), translating selections from the Argentinian Modernist poet Alfonsina Storni. His work has appeared in periodicals such as *Callaloo*, *Image*, *Harvard Review*, *Hudson Review*, *North American Review*, and *Southern Review*.

The recipient of a 2009 Literature Fellowship from the NEA and of the 2012 Prairie Schooner Book Prize, Menes frequently grounds explorations of poverty, exploitation, political upheaval, gender roles, human cruelty, and human tenderness within autobiographical contexts, turning to memory as a revealer of truths. In poems described by former US Poet Laureate Juan Felipe Herrera as "luscious, jeweled, intoxicating, fragrant as copál and sharp as obsidian," Menes often deploys paradox and irony as means of dramatizing the complexities of the heart, guiding readers into a liminal space, a border ground, in which conflicting visions encounter each other. Similarly, his style modulates between a kind of photographic realism and an exquisitely musical lyricism, just as his frequently bilingual poems move between English and Spanish. As Menes has said of his own work, "I have a passion for amalgamation, not just as a trope but as a way of thinking, a style of living." Indeed, not only is Menes adept in multiple poetic genres and forms, but his subjects are also various, including history, syncretic religion, geography, ethnography, and theology. However, despite their wide-ranging meditations, the poems are consistently grounded in concrete experience. As Charles Harper Webb writes, "These delectable poems beg to be tasted. To be spoken. To be sung."

Selected Bibliography
Rumba atop the Stones (2001); *Furia* (2005); *Fetish* (2013); *Heresies* (2015); *Memoria* (2019); *The Gospel of Wildflowers and Weeds* (2022)

MIAMI, SOUTH KENDALL, 1969

Papá was hosing down our new silver
Grand Prix, I scrubbing muddy floor mats,
when seven boys rode up
our driveway, legs tommy-gunned by mosquitoes,
eyes gunpowder blue.

They formed a line, passing around
a furry bowie knife.
Go back to Cuba, the chorus taunted.
We hate the Spanish.

Indigo snake coiled about his wrist,
Marcus hissed, snarled, telling my father
to kiss his ass. *Besamacula.*[19]

A fellow fifth-grader, it was Marcus who'd pounce
on me as I walked home from school,
calling me a dumb spic for saying *yellow*
like *jell-o*, bony arms choking, my mouth scrubbed
in dirt of dandelion and bitterweed.

I cried alone in my room, ashamed
for not hitting back, praying for Marcus's death,
fists pummeling the pillow; Papá warned
I'd grow up queer if I couldn't fistfight
like my younger brother Carlos, "little rooster."

The boys began to hoot,
make monkey faces, Marcus playacted
a lynching with the snake.
Papá charged, spraying water, shouting *I cole
de polís, foqui sanambambiches.*[20]

---

19 Slightly garbled Spanish for the previous words in the line.
20 Slightly garbled English for "I'll call the police," followed by a curse.

Then all seven mounted their bicycles,
sprinting toward avocado
groves; some days later we found death's-
heads carved on the garage door.

Papá sold the house at a loss, and we moved
to a bungalow off Calle Ocho,
our neighbors newly arrived refugees.

By 1971 Freedom Flights
were bringing hundreds of Cubans
each day, my grandmother Nena
among them; the Everglades dredged
for an expanding Little Havana,
políticos dreaming of
Malecón[21] on Biscayne Bay.

Stars and Stripes
flying from car antennas,
hate signs taped to windows,
Anglos fled to rural Manatee
and Osceola, some journeying
as far north as Alachua,
Apalachicola Bay, Blackwater River;
and County Line Road,
a strip of gravel and sticks,
the new border dividing
America from América.

2005

---

21 The Malecón is broad roadway and seawall along the coast in Havana, Cuba.

Sharing a Meal with the Cuban Ex-Political Prisoners

Colony Hotel, South Miami Beach, 1993

A pileup of black pots, clay pans on a tile table,
nine guests cramped on low stools—
milk crates—cold drinks between our legs to calm

the tiny man who'd been tortured.
with ice water, another guy, phobic of things
metallic, using a plastic spork from 7-Eleven.

The fried pork is suck-to-the-bone good, but I quit
eating when Saúl, our host, fiancée's classmate,
starts to describe his years at La Cabaña[22]
where he lost one kidney to pesticides in the well,

one eye spooned out, liver stuck with knitting needles.
How time got lost without clocks, bells,
calendars, roosters, his own heartbeat in disarray.

Just as I take the fork again, Saúl expounds
on pain, his power to numb nerves, gums, joints,
stretch skin like a rubber sail, harden the skull
to titanium. More men tell their stories of rape

by German shepherds in hospital rooms,
having to march wearing wool socks with glass,
the loud machine that took out toenails.

I cannot stop sweating, shaking, fiancée poking,
what's wrong with you, show respect,
these men are brave, which makes me more nervous.
I swoon in the bathroom, my skull pains

---

22 La Fortaleza de San Carlos de la Cabaña is an eighteenth-century fortress on the east side of
Havana, used as a prison during the Castro regime.

with their screams, throbbing image of a little man
frantic in a ballroom of funhouse mirrors,
convex phantasms, gun pops, flush of voices,
his head butting glass to make the nightmare stop.

2019

THE MAXIMUM LEADER ADDRESSES HIS ISLAND NATION

For half a century we have triumphed at war and insurrection, our legions
victorious across the continents. The capitalist hordes succumb like ants
to our Katyushas & Kalashnikovs.[23] Our breath is napalm, our sweat
nitroglycerin, our children's lullaby Fatherland or Death. Despite these
martial glories, we are a poor island between the Tropics of Cancer and
Capricorn. Winds betray us in the rainy season, droughts curse every
nine years. Why should geography imprison us? I hereby decree that we
are no longer tropical. Cut down the palms, my countrymen. Raze the
mangroves. Uproot the papaya trees. Let barbwire brambles cover our
valleys, steel conifers with grenades line our boulevards. After burning
down the corn fields, dredging the rice sloughs, trampling every manioc
hollow, you will sow rye with gunpowder, seed barley in bombshells.
Because life is not a carnival but a wake of reason, you will not tell spicy
jokes, play dominoes, or gyrate to drums. The polka will be our national
dance, all food boiled and bland. Our homes will have fireplaces and no
fans, windows sealed, verandas torn, parasols outlawed. You will wear wool
coats and sheepskin boots, long johns, ear muffs too. Whoever faints or
complains will be shot on sight. I will institute a ten-year plan in which
every scientist and sorcerer will wage war on the tropics. Meanwhile you
will walk through drifts of plastic snow, dry-ice cobbles, pretending to
shiver, pretending that breath freezes in air, pretending that arctic winds
crackle your face.

2013

---

23 The Katyusha is a rocket-launcher; the Kalashnikov is an automatic rifle. Both weapons were
manufactured by the Soviet Union.

DEN OF THE LIONESS

An outcast since her release from political prison,
she lives on a rooftop next to a rain barrel,
raising chickens and growing tomatoes in cans
freckled with rust, her one-room house
built without screws or nails, a troweled gruel
of cement, sawdust, glass shards, the zinc roof
so hot gulls avoid it in the early afternoon.

As the journalist walks inside her door,
a small window glares like a Cyclops' eye.
Buenas tardes, he stutters, as if his tongue
had sprained. Her floor tilts when he sits
on a vinyl couch with jiggly chrome legs,
its honeycomb of holes fixed with wax.
Family photos in Styrofoam frames hang
from mildewed walls; a milk-bottle aquarium
rests on a table made from bowed planking.

Details get jotted hurriedly. He turns on
the tape recorder, and the woman tells stories
of teaching sharecroppers to read, write
in the cane fields of Villa Clara,[24] her pride
wearing the militia's olive-green uniform,
how she broke a horse, slaughtered a pig,
thatched a hut. He cuts in, blurts *por favor*,
hand held up like a stop sign, says it's her
long imprisonment he's come to write about.
Readers want tragedy not happy pastorals.

She starts to weep, body crouching.
He flinches, then clutches her hand,
offering rum from his knapsack.
The rolling capstan continues to whirr
as she recalls those thirteen years

24 Villa Clara is a province in the north-central portion of Cuba.

inside a cell the size of a broom closet,
a prison called Den of the Lioness,
where each day she ate boiled feed
dyed to look like grits, drank sewage
guards joked was chocolate milk,
tag-team beatings with electrical wire,

midnight firing squads that faked
her execution, harrowing hours
hung upside down from an empty well,
yet how despite all this suffering
she kept sane tending God's creatures
like St. Francis of Assisi, a lame rat
one night, a pregnant mouse another,
the croaking frog, the chirping cricket.

2013

Palma y Jagüey

Valley of Yumurí:[25] a royal palm
prey of a strangler fig—
roots coiled around like a swarm
of snakes. "Miraculous how
la palma resists *el jagüey*,"[26]
I tell Omar, my wife's uncle.
Shaggy fronds wiggle rumbas;
the trunk erect, robust.
Along the road many are crooked,
stumped, lopped at the crown.

---

25 The Yumurí is a Cuban river whose valley lies in the western province of Matanzas.
26 "*Jagüey*: Cuban name of the strangler fig." – Menes's note

"A living metaphor,"
I declare. "Cuba will survive
communism, even if it constricts
her forty more years."
"Metaphor is all words,
and we distrust everything that
sounds pretty," Omar replies,
flicking his cigarette
into a cluster of palm nuts.
"Every peasant knows
el jagüey is treacherous.
La palma will die,
for nature doesn't care
what we think or feel."

The sun ignites
and we sit beneath the shade.
Hills muffle sea wind,
clouds shrink. Omar scoops
red earth, grains crumbling
between chapped fingers,
puts a wet lump
in my hand. "This rich earth
bears nothing," he says.
"Whether sweet or bitter,
words will not fill our bellies.
Your *palmita* does not represent
victory. Look how alone
it is between these limestone hills,
abandoned by its kind—
so gregarious a tree
you see whole flocks perched
on hills sunbathing,
wind preening their plumes."

A flock of *negritos*—
black finches—swarms *la palma*
to drink morning rain
that nestles in leaf nodes,
gorge on ripe figs
whose tiny seeds
their swollen bellies
will scatter in other valleys,
hollows, clearings,
as if *jagüey* knew
the instinct of birds,
the physics of flight.

2005

WREATH OF DESERT LILIES

road to Jorge Chávez International Airport, Lima, 1980s

Jets etch lead skies, diesels drone, smokestacks spew dust
That palls pickers' huts, scrapped tin, thatch of broken brooms.
Boys dig up balls, girls cull dolls to mend. Down flumes
Of debris, household scrub, they shoot gulls, slings that gust
Round stones. The mother harrows by tar ponds, rust
Swales, and thinks of home, its rich soil, ice lakes, coca blooms.
War made her flee to these dunes where hunger looms
Despite hard work or faith, but still she prays to Mary's bust
For rains that never come, just winter's metallic mist,
Nor does Christ return, so old tires bake to wheels of bread.
Those rare times Lenten light can pierce the steel haze,
Her spirits improve, joints don't ache, and she'll wrest
Open the white box beneath a rebar cross, its small bed
Of rubber roses, and hold shoes, clothes, locks soft as maize
                                Silk, first daughter's, born in May's
Calcareous light, the happy child who taunted death

With a weak heart. At age six when she drew her last breath
                     The mother braided a wreath,
Desert lilies, but kept it, hung from a cross, to recall
Daughter's grace, soft poise, as she culled the refuse shoal.

                                    2015

CASTIZO

Centuries ago when the Inquisition
scoured Spain for every secret Jew
or Muslim, people hung sausages,
salted bacon from their thresholds
to prove they were *castizo*,
people of good stock, old Christians
going back three generations.

Blood purity obsessed my mother
not out of pride but rather
from the shame of being impure,
the great-granddaughter
on her mom's side of a Chinese coolie,
making her extol her Catalan father
to the point of believing
he descended from a long line
of hidalgos like Don Quijote,

which leads me to another
Spanish prejudice, the one against
manual labor, also strangely
tied to blood purity. An hidalgo[27]
would never work with his hands
even if it meant wearing rags
and eating cold beans with moldy bread,

---

27 An "hidalgo" was a member of the Spanish nobility.

as opposed to the moriscos,
Muslim converts, who excelled
in agriculture, manual crafts.

"Don't ever work with your hands,"
Mamá would say. "Go to college.
Become a lawyer or an engineer."
To her a manual laborer was ignorant,
brutish, loathsome, no matter how good
a living he might make for his family.

When my father lost his fortune
in the furniture business
and had to go back to being a workman,
a maker of kitchen cabinets,
in a small rented garage near Hialeah,[28]
Mamá lost all respect for him,
complaining of his crude jokes,
rustic manners, hideous farts,
his nasty habit of taking a shower
with his socks and underwear.

"Don't be a failure like your father,"
she'd warn, and though I'd been bookish
from a young age, it was this fear
that nudged me toward college.

Forgive me, Mamá, but all handiwork
is charged with grace. Our hands,
more than our feet, root us to the world.
It is the hand that draws a bird,
scores a requiem, writes an elegy.

2019

---

28 A city in Miami-Dade County, Florida.

Juancito's Wake

Lost Grove Squatters' Camp, Lima, 1985

Over white vinyl, Rosa sets silver
candlesticks (rented), tinplate crucifixes—
five solder wounds—son's coffin
trembling on crippled legs when an old truck
rumbles past these desert shacks,

cardboard & reed mats tied to sticks.
Daughter Rosita crosses herself the Spanish
way, kissing the thumb when done,
pins purple-cloth medals of El Niño Jesús,
a burial gown sewn from rice sacking.

Mourners will come with egg-bread angels,
Our Lord of Sorrows' pudding—purple corn—
for the afterlife; most are live-out maids
like Rosa, the rest laundresses who twist shirts
until they surrender those last waterdrops

too precious for dirt, saved in oil drums
used to wash dishes & newborns. Dead from
hunger, Juancito is the third child she's lost
since coming from Ancash, highland province
in *la mancha india*, Perú's poorest.

They pose in Sunday's clothes, Rosa stoic,
dignified; in the background a road map
of Perú, one square clock that doesn't work.
Juancito's rubbery hands hold daisies,
shredded newspaper smelling of fish meal.

I take out a can from my bandoleer,
shoot from angles, cropping for dramatic
composition. Images freeze in silver;

flash mummifies. "Third World people
are real," customers say

as they buy $1,000 prints—poster size
Agfa sepia, Cibachrome color—to be hung
beneath track lights, Bal Harbour & South Beach
condos. The last reel shot, I thank Rosa,
handing her rubber-banded bills

she buries inside a broken bottle
of *pisco*[29] shaped like an Inca figurine.
"It's for her I struggle. Already she knows
how to read & write, do arithmetic."
Holding the sheet-metal door open,

Rosita rubs rheum off black eyes
like wilted grapes—asks, "In your
country are there many poor like
here?" "Poverty is relative," I answer
stupidly, leaving her puzzled.

Girls hopscotch along hedgerows
of barbed wire, runts bark at garbage sparks.
I return to the hotel, the cab having waited two
hours. "These are the children God forgot,"
cabbie says, hissing away barefoot boys,

shoe-shine boxes strapped to their backs,
pockets bulging with rags that buff leather
into obsidian mirrors. Yelling *señor,
señor*, they run through a wake
of dust, the incense of cloudless skies.

2013

---

29 "Pisco: A type of Peruvian brandy." – Menes's note.

Timothy Murphy (1951–2018)

Timothy Murphy was born in Hibbing, Minnesota, in 1951. In 1972, he graduated from Yale University, where he studied under the great poet and novelist Robert Penn Warren, who told him, "Go home, boy. Buy a farm. Sink your toes in that rich soil and grow some roots." After graduation, Murphy worked for the Connecticut General Life Insurance's office in Minneapolis before purchasing a farm near Gwinner, North Dakota, in 1982. Ultimately, he would become a venture capitalist and the managing partner of several farms in and around the Red River Valley. Living outside of academia, Murphy was in no hurry to publish his work, and his first book, *The Deed of Gift*, collected poems written over a span of twenty years. Subsequently, the books would come rapidly, including, in addition to volumes of original verse, *Set the Ploughshare Deep: A Prairie Memoir* (2000) and a translation of *Beowulf* (2004), completed with his partner of many years, Alan Sullivan. Quickly acclaimed by several prominent poets, Murphy's work appeared in periodicals such as *Commonweal, First Things, Gray's Sporting Journal, Hudson Review, The New Criterion, Poetry*, and *The Sewanee Review*.

In his preface to Murphy's first book, former US Poet Laureate Richard Wilbur wrote, "A reader will find . . . that the poems are slender and on the whole brief; and he will also find them to be resourcefully rhymed. A further finding, which the reader will make at once, is that despite the technical challenges which Murphy sets himself and meets, the voice of the poem is not that of a daredevil formalist or nifty technician, rather it is the voice of a Dakota farmer who knows everything about outrageous extremes of weather, crop failure, and the many adversities which can lead to falling-down barns and ghost towns." At times resembling the work of Regionalist poets such as Ted Kooser, Byron Herbert Reece, or Robert Francis, Murphy's best poems compress and distill local experiences to reveal abiding truths in the manner of Emily Dickinson and Robert Frost. And yet, for all their devotion to the Great Plains and the inhabitants thereof, Murphy's poems are also frequently inflected with a Classical touch, reminiscent, at times, of Catullus or Martial. Capable of bawdiness and good humor as well as of profound religious devotion, Murphy brings wit and technical acuity to bear on a rural life given largely to hunting and farming.

Selected Bibliography
The Deed of Gift (1998); *Very Far North* (2002); *Mortal Stakes / Faint Thunder* (2011); *Hunter's Log* (2011); *Devotions* (2017); *Hunter's Log II & III* (2019); *Hiking All Night* (2021); *Last Poems* (2021)

THE TRACK OF A STORM

Bastille Day, 1995

We grieve for the twelve trees we lost last night,
pillars of our community, old friends
and confidants dismembered in our sight,
stripped of their crowns by the unruly winds.
There were no baskets to receive their heads,
no women knitting by the guillotines,
only two sleepers rousted from their beds
by fusillades of hailstones on the screens.
Her nest shattered, her battered hatchlings drowned,
a stunned and silent junko[30] watches me
chainsawing limbs from corpses of the downed,
clearing the understory of debris
while supple saplings which survived the blast
lay claim to light and liberty at last.

1998

CASE NOTES

for Dr. Richard Kolotkin

3/7/02

Raped at an early age
by older altar boy.
"Damned by the Church to Hell,
never to sire a son,
perhaps man's greatest joy,"
said father in a rage.
Patient was twenty-one.
Handled it pretty well.

---

30 The "junko" here is the "junco," a type of sparrow.

3/14/02

Curiously, have learned
patient was Eagle Scout.
Outraged that Scouts have spurned
each camper who is 'out.'
Questioned if taunts endured
are buried? "No, immured."

3/21/02

Allured by verse and drink
when he was just sixteen,
turned to drugs at Yale.
Patient began to think
people would see a 'queen'—
scrawny, friendless, frail—
a 'queer' condemned to fail.

4/1/02

Into a straight town
he brought a sober lover.
"Worked smarter, drank harder
to stock an empty larder,"
wrote poetry, the cover
for grief he cannot drown.

4/9/02

Uneasy with late father,
feared for by his mother,
lover, and younger brother.
Various neuroses,
but no profound psychosis.
Precarious prognosis.

2011

HUNTING TIME

for R.S. Gwynn

It's not just dirt-cheap prices,
diseases in our herds
or the global banking crisis.
Our fields are beset by birds.
Gwynn slips in a cartridge,
and another shell is pinned—
poets and dogs and partridge
all working into the wind.

The raptor is our fellow
predator of the air.
We humans lack his yellow
iris, his slitted stare;
but Brownings[31] are as deadly
as dripping beak or claw,
and our prey bleeds as redly
as rodent eaten raw.

Though nowadays a shooter
keeps impulse under lock,
my old Kentucky tutor
once shot and stuffed a hawk.
He told me time was reckoned
by the crippled bird's last breath
as the marksman spared a second
to practice for his death.[32]

2002

---

31 The "Brownings" here are, literally, rifles. A pun—suggesting Robert and Elizabeth Barrett Browning, English poets of Victorian England, and perhaps poets more generally—is possible.
32 The "old Kentucky tutor" is Robert Penn Warren. The tale of his shooting and stuffing a hawk may be found in Warren's poem "Red-Tailed Hawk and the Pyre of Youth." The final line of this poem alludes to Warren's early poem, "Bearded Oaks."

THE BLIND

Gunners a decade dead
wing through my father's mind
as he limps out to the blind
bundled against the wind.

By some ancestral code
fathers and sons don't break,
we each carry a load
of which we cannot speak.

Here we commit our dead
to the unyielding land
where broken windmills creak
and stricken ganders cry.

Father, the dog and I
are learning how to die
with our feet stuck in the muck
and our eyes trained on the sky.

                    1998

JASPER LAKE

Perched on a granite peak
where golden eagles shriek
my love and I peer down
watching the Rockies drown—
crag and evergreen
sunk in aquamarine.
Over the lake last night
speckled trout took flight,

leaping the mirrored moon.
Now in the warmth of noon
gullied glaciers groan,
pouring silt and stone
into the seething streams.
Brief! Brief! a marmot screams,
diving under the scree
as its mountain heads for the sea.

1998

THE REVERSION

Born to go astray,
I fled the Catholic fold
when I was twelve years old,
a lamb who ran away,
prey to the wolves, the cold.

My shepherd piped me home.
Filing into a pew,
I learned what Caesar knew:
all roads lead to Rome
where wolves are mothers too.[33]

2011

---

33 Romulus and Remus, legendary founders of Rome as recorded in the Roman historian Livy, were raised by wolves.

CROSS-LASHED

A chapel, not a church:
just a clearing in the wood
of aspen, pine and birch,
where a rude altar stood

pegged by a boy's hands;
behind it a birchwood cross
cross-lashed, but neither stands.
They are gone under the moss.

When I quit Wilderness Camp[34]
I rose up from my knees
and left the altar lamp
burning in the trees.

Summits would loom above
the stony trails I trod.
Sex led me to love;
love bound me to God.

2011

---

34 Camp Wilderness, located near Park Rapids, MN, has long been a prominent campground for Scouts.

SOUL OF THE NORTH

Out of my depth, I pray.
Bound as I was at birth
to fish, to hunt the earth
and find my northern way,
I mutter, "I have sinned,"
wander the wild grass,
flourish awhile and pass
whistling into the wind.

As char swim to the clear
tundra rivers that run
under the midnight sun,
as wolves follow the deer
drawn from ford to ford,
as clamorous geese in V's
throng to the thawing seas—
all creatures of one accord—
my soul thirsts for the Lord.

2011

Alfred Nicol (1956)

Born in Amesbury, Massachusetts, Alfred Nicol was the second of four children in a working-class French-Canadian family. His father was a foreman in a sheet metal shop. Of his mother, who died when he was fourteen, Nicol says she worked at a hat factory and "was a tireless housewife, sleeping no more than 5 hours a night. She baked all of the bread we ate; she made all of our clothes." Though Nicol's parents were not highly educated, they encouraged his studies. After graduation from Dartmouth College, with a brief stint at The Jack Kerouac School of Disembodied Poetics at the Naropa Institute, Nicol worked as a farmhand, a poet-in-the-schools, a house painter, and, for twenty years, as a pressman in the printing industry.

Through the years Nicol continued to write, and in 1999, he joined the Powow River Poets, a collective of accomplished formalist poets in Newburyport, Massachusetts. Though Nicol had been primarily working in free verse, he began trying his hand at received forms, and his subsequent poems are noteworthy for his mastery of poetic craft. Of his first collection, *Winter Light*, which received the 2004 Richard Wilbur Award, Jay Parini writes, "Nicol is naturally drawn toward the affirming limits of formal poetry, but there is an uncanny freedom in this work—a willingness to take large emotional risk, writing about the most basic human emotions with an icy clarity. On every page Nicol exhibits a genuine largeness of spirit and grace of mind."

In addition to his three poetry collections, Nicol edited *The Powow River Anthology*, published in 2006, and has written the lyrics for nine original compositions by classical/flamenco guitarist John Tavano for a CD entitled *The Subtle Thread*. With Tavano and the poet Rhina Espaillat, he recorded *Melopoeia*, a CD of poetry recited with musical accompaniment. His work has been published in many journals, including *Commonweal*, *The Formalist*, *Rattapallax*, and *New England Review*. Nicol lives in West Newbury, Massachusetts.

Selected Bibliography
Poems: *Winter Light* (2004); *Elegy for Everyone* (2009); *Animal Psalms* (2016).
Collaborations: *Second Hand Second Mind: Dreams and Photographs by Alfred Nicol and Elise Nicol* (2011); *Brief Accident of Light*, co-written with Rhina Espaillat (2019).

ELEGY FOR EVERYONE

It's best to read the obituaries first.
Wonderful people die most every day,
people you may only know in passing
but that was always true of everyone.
I read today of Sister Joan Margaret,
whose heart gave out. She is so lovely
in her photograph, although it's jagged,
probably a download from the Web,
which makes it seem ephemeral and frail
and easily compared to life itself,
unless you think of everlasting life.
She wasn't one to have her picture taken;
they used the one they had, in which she's not
alone, which is itself remarkable.
They usually crop the others from the photo.
But she is with a girl who's nine or ten.
It is a joy to see—although to say
that she is lovely gives the wrong impression:
"Short and square," is how she is described.
What's more, there is a tooth that shows itself
too prominently in her aged mouth
when she is smiling, as she is smiling here.
That's what made me look again, to see
the perfect match they made, the pretty girl
in Haiti mischievously grinning back
missing that very tooth in her own smile.
They clearly take delight in one another—
What is it makes the self one goes around in
such a complement to other selves?

A hurricane has flooded the main road.
There is an infant floating on a table,
and here comes Sister Joan—driving a jeep!
She hikes up her nun's habit and wades out
to rescue Gertie Gay, orphaned in the storm,

whom she will raise, and who will speak today
in Roxbury at her memorial.
The happy ending makes it comedy,
as even death is rendered comic
by the Resurrection. No wonder they can laugh.
That is a cross of black enameled wood
she's wearing on her chest. It's not an "S."

It's best to read the obituaries first,
before the news and sports. They're better written.
It comes of knowing rules of composition,
especially *Beginning Middle End.*
Sister Joan was ninety-nine years old.
Her story's got a lot of middle to it.
There is a man called Jo-Jo, a fine artist.
She had him fitted with limbs, years ago;
he had been just a torso of a boy.
With her it's literal that the self should find
completion in the other. She knew herself.
She'd been adopted when her mother died
shortly after giving birth to her.
She knew first hand before she learned to speak
the stranger's palm cradling her infant head,
and knew by heart a thing the Bible taught,
having felt its truth before she read
religion undefiled before the Father
is this: to visit the fatherless.
                           Odd phrasing—
almost as if the Father is the father
who is missing and who will be pleased
if we should visit his abandoned children.

Sister Joan built a school for the disabled,
which started in a crèche beneath a tree.
At first there were three children gathered there,
one blind, one deaf, the other someway crippled.
She must have borrowed blindness from the child,
tried on the other's deafness not to hear

how greatly overmatched she'd always be;
she learned the cripple's way of going forward;
she studied where to lean.

Today three-hundred-sixty handicapped
attend St. Vincent's School in Port-au-Prince.
I think of all the hundreds unenrolled,
the endless repetition of mistakes
the Maker makes, from which you'd think he'd learn.
Unless we are to think he's only human;
and so she drives a Jeep around the country
in his service, picking up what's fallen,
laughing with the broken ones. No,
her god I think is wholly one of us
but something more—a vital something more.

Only human doesn't get things done,
not the things that matter. Only human
sends a check and gets a calendar.
Only human gets enthusiastic
now and then. It never lasts. So what.
The things that matter always take forever.
Only human hasn't time for that.

2009

A WAGE-EARNER'S LAMENT

The man whose greeting passed for praise,
With whom I traded time for bread,
The man I fought to get a raise,
The man who bought my days, is dead.

And shall I start before the dawn,
And work till after day is done,
Laboring still when he is gone,
So neither of us sees the sun?

The man to whom I sold my days
Has taken them beneath the earth.
Where in those dark and narrow ways
Will he find gold of equal worth?

2009

THE GIFT

Quick as thought, the shortstop dives to snag
the blur of white, and though he's on his knees,
his strong peg beats the runner to the bag.
The gifted do what's difficult with ease.

Such music is clear water over stones.
So fluid are her hands upon the keys,
there springs a braided stream of sparkling tones.
The gifted do what's difficult with ease.

The couples link their arms along the pier,
whispering under lanterns in the breeze.
Some few small words fall softly on the ear.
The gifted do what's difficult with ease.

2009

WHY BEES HUM

The ancients say that Zeus so loved the bees
he made them golden like the sun,
imparting to each one
a ray of sacred fire, finely spun—
bright scarves in which they wouldn't freeze
when winter bared the trees.

Freed from the mortal fear of winter time,
whose threat the god had stooped to lift,
and grateful for the gift,
the bees spread out through autumn fields to drift
among the flowers, or cling and climb
and sip of the sublime

unhurried and unworried. Given heat,
they celebrate by making something sweet.

2016

Angela Alaimo O'Donnell (1960)

Angela Alaimo O'Donnell was born in Wilkes-Barre, Pennsylvania, and grew up in the small town of West Wyoming, Pennsylvania, one of five children raised by a young, widowed mother. A graduate of Penn State University, she holds a Master's and a PhD in English Language & Literature from the University of North Carolina at Chapel Hill. In addition to her eleven poetry collections, she has written a memoir about caring for her dying mother, and four books about Flannery O'Connor—a literary biography, a critical work, a book of poems that channel O'Connor's voice, and a book of hours. O'Donnell has received multiple awards for her prose works from the Catholic Press Association and won the Paraclete Poetry award for her book *Holy Land*.

O'Donnell writes formally adept poems that are simultaneously grounded in daily experience and concerned with Catholic spirituality, poems that are, in the poet's own words, "deeply incarnational, focused on the body and the physicality of being, on sacramental moments that reveal connections between the human and the divine." As Thomas Lynch has written, "If rhyme and meter are, as [Seamus] Heaney said, the table manners of the language arts, then Angela Alaimo O'Donnell has set out a sumptuous feast, if not bardic, then beatific, recalling a time when pilgrims knew to spread good word by heart."

O'Donnell lives in Bronxville, New York. A professor at Fordham University in New York City, she serves as Associate Director of the Curran Center for American Catholic Studies. O'Donnell writes essays on the relationship of literature and art to the Catholic intellectual tradition. A columnist for the Jesuit magazine *America*, she contributes essays devoted to books and culture. Among the many publications in which her poems have appeared are *America*, *Potomac Review*, *Christian Century*, *Mezzo Cammin*, and *Italian Americana*.

Selected Bibliography
Poems: *Moving Houses* (2009); *Saint Sinatra* (2011); *Waking My Mother* (2013); *Lovers' Almanac* (2015); *Still Pilgrim* (2017); *Andalusian Hours: Poems from the Porch of Flannery O'Connor* (2020); *Love in the Time of Coronavirus* (2021); *Holy Land* (2022); *Dear Dante* (2024). Memoir: *Mortal Blessings: A Sacramental Farewell* (2014). Criticism: *Radical Ambivalence: Race in Flannery O'Connor* (2020).

OTHER MOTHERS

Other girls' mothers
sold *Avon, Bee-line, Tupperware.*[35]

My mother took lovers.
Young ones. Dark ones. True ones.

The kind that came back,
parked their cars in the drive,

and slept in our house
night after night after night.

Other girls' mothers
wore aprons, baked bread.

My mother slipped on stockings,
stepped into heels, and went to work

late evenings while we'd lie
half-awake in our beds.

We'd hope for peanuts, chips, mints,
small signs she'd remembered us.

Other girls' mothers
didn't like my mother,

grew green-eyed in the grocery,
cold-shouldered us at Mass

where she'd stay in the pew,
marooned, at Communion,

---

35 All three of the aforementioned were companies that afforded women sales positions, primarily
during the 1950s and 60s.

her black mantilla
shadowing her black eyes.

Other girls' mothers
liked their daughters,

asked them questions,
listened for replies.

My mother would have thought
them amusing

had she thought
of other mothers at all.

2009

Now & At the Hour of Our Death

for Will

Because he spoke across a thousand miles,
Because she breathed her last breaths,
Because she was deep in her opium sleep
    And we were not,
I held the phone to my dying mother's ear.

Because he said he missed her,
Because it was true,
Because the last human voice she heard
    Said *I love you,*
Our mother's heart rested at 10:38.

Because joy never comes too late.

2013

WATCHING *DIRTY DANCING* WITH MY MOTHER

in the sad sleep of the nursing home,
we are both surprised by beauty alone,

by Jennifer's new-found ecstasy,
the passion of young Patrick Swayze

as he glides her across the bare wood,
lifts her high towards the old god of girlhood

and sets her down, sure of her charm
each step beyond his circling arms.

Nothing can soothe her father's frown
seeing his daughter as *someone* now,

no more the child she cannot stay.
Patrick, too, has since passed away.

None of us the beauty we used to be,
my mother, those dancers, me.

2013

SAINT SINATRA[36]

"Saints are the most excellent of voices,
the most brilliant of stars." *Avery Cardinal Dulles*

Croon to me, Baby,
blue-eyes smiling,

---

36 Frank Sinatra was a popular singer and actor whose career ran from the mid-1930s to the mid-1990s.

So *Easy to Love*
Night and Day,

skinny legs draped
in gabardine as you sway

sweet and easy, singing.
The mike your attribute,

lucky close to those lips,
In other words, baby, kiss me.

I've Got a Crush on You, Sweetie Pie,
You, Sicilian Saint of Song,

the one girls pray to when we lie
awake, pictures of boys in our heads,

each of them holy-card pretty as you
only *In the Blue of Evening.*

You and the Night and the Music
much more than we can stand,

we fall to our knobby knees,
genuflect to your smooth

slide down the scale of desire,
a true tune we know and can't carry.

O Hoboken Hero of Eros,
Star-eyed *Stranger in the Night,*

Pray for us, Sinner. Sing us alive.
Take these Valentine hearts from our hands.

2011

Sunrise in Sicily

Etna's smoking and the sky's on fire,
province of the lord of light.
First fierce color, then sweet heat,
the ready rise of blinding white.
What beauty rules the westing day?
What future bodes so broad and blue?
Thick night thins and wisps away
and lends these hours to me and you.

So, love, what shall we do with it—
the pearl that's placed in our own hands
plucked from some dark oyster bed,
palmed miracle of sea and sand.
The round perfection of the thing
enough to make the sun god sing.

2015

Kiki Petrosino (1970)

Kiki Petrosino is the author of *White Blood: a Lyric of Virginia* (2020) and three other poetry books, all from Sarabande. She holds graduate degrees from the University of Chicago and the University of Iowa Writer's Workshop. Her memoir, *Bright*, was released from Sarabande in 2022. She directs the Creative Writing Program at the University of Virginia, where she is a Professor of Poetry. Petrosino is the recipient of a DeWitt Wallace/Readers Digest fellowship from MacDowell artist residency, a Pushcart Prize, a Fellowship in Creative Writing from the National Endowment for the Arts, the UNT Rilke Prize, & the Spalding Prize, among other honors.

Petrosino's poems are formally inventive and wide-ranging, and she often approaches serious subjects with an inviting sense of play. Her collection *Fort Red Border*—the book's title being an anagram of the name "Robert Redford"—includes a section of poems spoken by a woman romantically involved with the actor. *Witch Wife* contains a pantoum, a sestina, and many villanelles or variations on that form. Petrosino's most recent collection, *White Blood: A Lyric of Virginia*, an exploration of her genealogical roots, includes both a double crown sonnet and erasure poetry based on her DNA testing results.

As Harryette Mullin has written, "Petrosino delights in unsettling the familiar with startling results, whether channeling Anne Sexton or William Blake. Her stylish innovation refashions traditional forms that insist on repetition." And Terrance Hayes says, "Kiki Petrosino has been perfecting a form of weaponized valentine, a love poem armed with play and appraisal, ever since her amazing debut. Her poems charm and fillet."

Selected Bibliography

Poems: *Fort Red Border* (2009); *Hymn for the Black Terrific* (2013); *Witch Wife* (2017); *Black Genealogy* (2017); *White Blood: A Lyric of Virginia* (2020). Memoir: *Bright* (2022).

Young

After Anne Sexton

A thousand pilot lights ago
when I'm a teenager half-gone to flab
in a low ranch house crammed
with ribboned handicrafts in January
I go pulling all the false candy canes
from the stale mulch out front
clown-sun blinking whitely over me
my bedroom window an ear
painted shut to keep the calliope of dreams
from sounding. Nearby, the Douglas Fir
thickens over older strings of lights, the chipped
blue bulbs & the gold, each wrapped in peeling floss
& held by keloids to the scruff
of an unloved trunk. Probably a million tiny
ice crystals drift on their rainbow way
while the feverish branches chafe & flake
& I, in my runny custard body
with its buried corkscrew of hate
tell the tree my story-songs
& think God can really hear
above the cold & snapping plastic canes
boots, belly, my dreams, what's wrong.

2017

The Shop at Monticello

I'm a black body in this Commonwealth, which turned black bodies
into money. Now, I have money to spend on little trinkets to remind me

of this fact. I'm a money machine & my body constitutes the common
wealth. I spend & spend in order to support this. I support this mountain
with my black money. Strange mountain in late bloom. Strange mansion
built on mountains of wealth. I spend so much, I'm late for the tour

where I'm a blooming black dollar sign. I look good in the Dome Room
prowling its high-gloss floor. It's common to desire such flooring

for my own home, but owning a home is still strange. My blackness
makes strange tools for a living, rakes the strangeness like dirt. I like to

rake my hands over merchandise: bayberry votives, English hyssop
in crisp sachets. I like this Engraved Pewter Bookmark so much suddenly

I line up for it, clenching my upright fist. I pay cash to prove myself
no shoplifter. Still, I abscond with my black feelings: crisp toast points

dunked in fig jam. On one hand, I must think very highly of myself
to come here. Then again, that sounds like something I would say.

2020

Souvenir

The glass lady doesn't know anything
about Sally Hemings except she was young
& got to live in Paris for two years. It doesn't
sound half bad, not when you think about it
straight-on, which nobody does, & *didn't
they dig up a jar of French cold cream near one of the cabins
out there?* The glass lady lifts candelabrum
after candelabrum in the shop whose windows
admit nothing but pewter sky. *She could've stayed
in France & been free, but instead she got right back
on that ship with him.* The glass lady's voice hums
with a harpsichord quality, just as she arrives
at *free will, she had it just like everyone.* Only now
I'm aware of the glass garden party hovering all
around us—pearl onions, champagne, & that sharp

makeup smell of grown ladies. *Isn't it really to his credit*
that she came back to live here? I feel my champagne
hatching its tiny mirrors. Perhaps it's the lady
who moves me. Amid the glass faces, I lift
my empty flute as if it's mine, as if I started it
as if I pulled, with hot tongs, a whole
orchid from the air.

2020

TWENTY-ONE

Journal, mixtape, leather coat.
Silk scarf painted with caducei.
Lunapark, broom flowers, ferryboat.
Ticket stub: Autobus 25.

Birthstone anklet, white Peugeot.
Journal, mixtape, leather coat.
Perseid shower, bear paw charm.
Lunapark, broom flowers, ferryboat.

Thumb ring, tank top, lucky coin.
Birthstone anklet, white Peugeot.
Pastasciutta, freckled arms.
Perseid shower, bear paw charm.

Campfire, windsurf, sudden wine.
Thumb ring, tank top, lucky coin.
Olive orchard, sunflower farm.
Pastasciutta, freckled arms.
Yogurt with apricots. Coca-Lite.
Campfire, sudden wine, windsurf.
Olive orchard, sunflower farm.
Laundry, terrace, Sting concert.

Feather earrings, volcano hike.
Yogurt, apricots, Coca-Lite.
Green-yellow sunset. Fever sleep.
Terrace. Laundry. Sting. Sting.

2017

LET ME TELL YOU PEOPLE SOMETHING

The women in my country, they are going into the yard with pots & spoons to bang at crows. Always, this. Because crows will eat every fruit from the trees, & then? Nothing left. So the women bang, they yell in a big voice every morning. But crow is not afraid of woman, it will come back tomorrow. Crow is like, you bring pot & spoon? I do not care. You know, *do not care?* Tomorrow, maybe, you leave this city. You take just one small box or one small case, fly to another house, put your box on the floor & ask: this box, who is it? Who lives in my house? You are forgetting all the time. I have seen you, wearing the name of your city on the T-shirts. Every name more huge, lying across the chest like a creature. Always, you complain in your small clothes. You complain when the rain is not stopping, but also: no rain. This complaining you do? Is just the ghost of the house you leave for another house. You don't remember. But. In my country, we take the young asparagus in March when it walks on the hills. Asparagus is like the persons we have loved, standing in the house of our parents. I am living here for many years now, but I do not forget my mother in the yard. My sister with her spoon. I do not weep in your way of ghosts. That's all.

2017

WITCH WIFE

I'll conjure the perfect Easter
& we'll plant mini spruces in the yard—
my pink gloves & your green gloves

like parrots from an opera over the earth—
We'll chatter about our enemies' spectacular deaths.
I'll conjure the perfect Easter

dark pesto sauce sealed with lemon
long cords of fusilli to remind you of my hair
& my pink gloves. Your gloves are green

& transparent like the skin of Christ
when He returned, filmed over with moss roses—
I'll conjure as perfect an Easter:

provolone cut from the whole ball
woody herbs burning our tongues—it's a holiday
I conjure with my pink-and-green gloves

wrangling life from the dirt. It all turns out
as I'd hoped. The warlocks of winter are dead
& it's Easter. I dig up body after body after body
with my pink gloves, my green gloves.

2017

Benjamin Alire Sáenz (1954)

Benjamin Alire Sáenz was born in Old Picacho, New Mexico, the fourth of seven children. When Sáenz was in the fourth grade, his parents lost their small cotton farm; afterward his father labored as a cement finisher, and his mother cleaned houses and worked in factories. Sáenz went to work, too, taking on various odd jobs, including picking onions and painting apartments.

After he graduated from high school, Sáenz studied at St. Thomas Seminary in Denver, drawn to the priesthood by Catholic leftists like Dorothy Day and Philip and Daniel Berrigan, and drawn also by the promise of an education he couldn't otherwise have afforded. After earning his BA from St. Thomas Seminary in Denver, Colorado, he studied at the University of Louvain in Belgium and returned to El Paso where he worked as a parish priest before realizing that writing was his true calling. Sáenz earned an MA in creative writing from the University of Texas at El Paso, started work toward a PhD at the University of Iowa, and was offered a Stegner Fellowship from Stanford University. In 1991 his first poetry collection received an American Book Award.

In addition to poetry, Sáenz also writes fiction for adults, teens, and children. Since 1994 he has taught in the creative writing program at the University of Texas at El Paso and has received multiple honors, including a Lannan Literary Award, the PEN/Faulkner Award for fiction and two Lambda Literary Awards. His books for young readers regularly sell in the tens of thousands.

Sáenz's poems are strongly informed by his Catholic upbringing. In his essay, "Notes from the City in Which I Live," Sáenz writes about his development as a poet: "Given my background, it wasn't surprising that, at first, I thought of poetry as some kind of sacred space, a confessional booth, a place where a sacrament took place, a place where I was cleansed if not forgiven, a place where I could see myself and the world more clearly." His work also vividly reflects El Paso's landscape, cultural history, and political realities, as well as his own personal struggles with addiction and trauma. As Luis Aleberto Urrea notes, "The work of Benjamin Alire Sáenz is rooted firmly on the border, in that space between the sacred and profane. He speaks for us all, and he speaks hard truths."

Selected Bibliography
Poems: *Calendar of Dust* (1991); *Dark and Perfect Angels* (1995); *Elegies in Blue* (2002); *Dreaming the End of War* (2006); *The Book of What Remains* (2010); *The Last Cigarette on Earth* (2017). Young Adult Novels: *Aristotle and Dante Discover the Secrets of the Universe* (2012); *Aristotle and Dante Dive Into the Waters of the World* (2021).

To the Desert

I came to you one rainless August night.
You taught me how to live without the rain.
You are thirst and thirst is all I know.
You are sand, wind, sun, and burning sky,
The hottest blue. You blow a breeze and brand
Your breath into my mouth. You reach—then *bend*
Your force, to break, blow, burn, and make me new.[37]
You wrap your name tight around my ribs
And keep me warm. I was born for you.
Above, below, by you, by you surrounded.
I wake to you at dawn. Never break your
Knot. Reach, rise, blow, *Sálvame, mi dios,*
Trágame, mi tierra. Salva, traga,[38] Break me,
I am bread. I will be the water for your thirst.

1995

Journeys

El Paso/Juárez
1984

Every day she crosses. She
has been here before, has passed these streets
so often she no longer notices the shops
nor their names nor the people. No longer
notices the officials at the bridge who let her
pass as if she were going shopping. They know
her, know where she's going, do not ask questions.
They have stopped smiling at each other.

---

37 From "Batter my Heart, three-person'd God," one of John Donne's *Holy Sonnets*.
38 "Save me, my God. Swallow me, my earth. Save, swallow." (Spanish).

Each morning she walks from her
Juárez home, crosses the bridge to El Paso.
Downtown, she waits for a bus that takes her
to a house where she irons and cleans and cooks.
She is not afraid to get caught. The Border
Patrol does not stop her as she waits for
the bus after work. They know what she does,
know she has no permit—but how would it look
arresting decent people's maids? How
would it look? And besides, she's a woman
getting old. The *Migra*[39] prefers to chase
young men. She no longer notices their green
vans. They do not exist for her.
Nor she, for them.

     She does not mind the daily journeys,
not far, and "really," she says to herself,
"it is all one city, Juárez and El Paso.
The river is small and tired. A border? Ha!"
She sits, she laughs, she catches her bus to go home.

     The woman whose house she cleans
asked her once if she wanted to be an American.
"No," she smiled, "I'm happy." What for,
she thought, what for? My children, they want
to live here. Not me. I belong in my Juárez.

     She cooks, she cleans, she takes her bus.
She journeys every day. The journey is easy,
never takes a long time, and always it is sunny.
When it rains, the people who live here
praise God—but she, she curses him
for the spit that soaks her skin.

1991

---

39 Immigration police

CREATION

Trinity Site, New Mexico
5:30 A.M., July 16, 1945

"Let there be light."
And there was light.

The sun was slow in arriving that morning
though it was no longer dark, was light enough,
and having been born with good eyes, we could see.
We stood on the cool cactus sand which was once
an ocean with a patience we rarely practiced.
It was hard to imagine so much water in this place
of permanent thirst. Motionless, we stood
just as we once waited for our sons to struggle
out of our wives. The labor wasn't long,
but the longest ten seconds of our lives. Ten
seconds, that was all—
        And then the man-made flash—
twice as large as the sun—photographed the moment
in fire. Flames burning the sands,
slashing the face of the calm.
        The ball of thunder strangled
the sky. Reached, blasted, bounced on rocks,
became a perfect tower—taller, wider, whiter
than the Aztecs ever dreamed of or desired.
All the gilded temples where we crossed ourselves
and worshipped perished in the smoke. Everything
surpassed in the new incense. Falling.
On our knees. It seemed to reach for us.
We prayed for it to stop, yet urged it on.
The air exploded hot, grew cold, then hot again
invoking Indian winds to rise, to blow,
to break the earth in half.
        Then it was silent.
Motionless, we stood—the air throwing us
back, and we remembered our selves, our past,

the boyhood houses filled with women's singing.
We rose, surveyed the aftermath of our great
experiment. There was not much damage:
rearranged sand, uprooted bushes, a few dead
rabbits. This was, after all, already a desert,
already named *Jornada del Muerto*,[40] plain
of the no-personed God.
      We had seen. And lived.
We blessed ourselves, smelling the victory.
We put on jubilant smiles in the face
of the outcome. But the smiles fell off
unable to withstand the great success.

      The sun was slow in arriving that morning.
Those of us who bore witness saw it rise
in the new sky, motionless, but it no longer
gave enough light. Now, after many years,
our eyes have grown accustomed to the dark.

        1991

AVENIDA JUÁREZ. MAY 7, 2010. 12:37 A.M.

Young soldiers, rifles slung over their shoulders, pace the dead and empty
street.

         *

Seven people laze out of the Kentucky Club, searching their pockets,
looking for change to pay the toll. Charon[41] does not take money from the
living—but the turnstile is hungry for coins. Sober in their drunkenness,
these ragged pilgrims place their quarters in the slots and begin their
journey home. They carry the weight of the evening, carry the weight of

---

40 Day of the Dead.
41 In Greek and Roman mythology, the ferryman who carries the souls of the dead across the
River Styx, into the realm of the dead.

this sad and singular thought: Juárez is no longer alive. Juárez is no longer alive.

*

The immigration agent checks the passport of a young woman. *What were you doing in Juárez? Do you have a death wish?* When he asks the next man in line if he has anything to declare, the man laughs: *I would like to declare my sadness. I would like to declare that all my dreams are dead.*

*

A man—alone—is making his way over the bridge. No hurry in his steps. He remembers another time, the streets full and teeming with commerce and expectation. He stares out into the lights of El Paso, his back to Juárez. He listens to the echoes of the empty streets. The laughter and dancing are gone. Nostalgia is his only consolation.

*

A handsome man, well-dressed, in his early thirties, rushes across the bridge. In twenty minutes he will be dancing in the nightclubs of El Paso. If the killings never stop, then neither does the dancing.

2017

Daniel Tobin (1958)

Daniel Tobin was born in Brooklyn, New York, in 1958. He graduated from Iona College in 1980 and earned a master's degree in theological studies from Harvard Divinity School in 1983. In 1990 he earned an MFA from the Low-Residency program at Warren Wilson College and completed a PhD in Religion and Literature at the University of Virginia in 1991. He taught at Carthage College from 1991 to 2002, and since 2002 he has taught at Emerson College in the Department of Writing, Literature, and Publishing. His work has received the Loftus Award for Outstanding Achievement in Arts & Letters, the Massachusetts Book Award, *The Discovery / The Nation* Award, the Robert Penn Warren Award, The Pushcart Prize, and the Stephen J. Meringoff Prize, and Tobin has also received a Guggenheim Fellowship, an NEA Fellowship, and a Robert Frost Fellowship. His book *Blood Labors* was named one of the Best Poetry Books of 2018 by *The New York Times*. Tobin's work appears in periodicals such as *Best American Poetry*, *The Hudson Review*, *The Kenyon Review*, *Paris Review*, *Poetry*, *The Times Literary Supplement*, *The Sewanee Review*, and *The Southern Review*.

Frequently, as Edward Hirsch has noted, "in quest of transcendence, in search of the sacred," Tobin's poetry is remarkably daring. While his 2005 book, *The Narrows*, merges personal memories of his childhood neighborhood in Brooklyn with mythic vision in a manner approaching the epic, his 2016 volume, *From Nothing*, explores physics and metaphysics with equal aplomb through the life of Georges Lemaître, the Jesuit priest whose work solved problems raised by Einstein's Theory of General Relativity and quantum mechanics. Moreover, *From Nothing* is only the first in a trilogy of books (the latter two focus on Simone Weil and Teilhard de Chardin, respectively) that explore the relationship between science and faith and are collected in *The Mansions*.

Nevertheless, Tobin's best work remains grounded in a familiar world, often deploying a nimble and almost acrobatic parataxis to discover unforeseen connections between the mundane and the divine mysteries. Indeed, equally capable of making luminous the domestic detail or the theological subtlety, Tobin's ambitious and accomplished verse justifies Eamonn Wall's boldly declaring, in regard to *The Narrows*, "The Robert Lowell Irish America has been waiting for has arrived."

Selected Bibliography
Poems: *Where the World Is Made* (1999); *Double Life* (2004); *The Narrows* (2005); *Second Things* (2008); *Belated Heavens* (2010); *The Net* (2014); *From Nothing* (2016); *Blood Labors* (2018); *The Mansions* (2023). Criticism: *Passage to the Center: Imagination and the Sacred in the Poetry of Seamus Heaney* (2009); *On Serious Earth: Poetry & Transcendence* (2019).

The Afterlife

What's worse, nearly, than the nothing you hope it's not
Is the thought of your many dead still nearby
Watching you from behind your life's one-way mirror.

They seem as they hover behind the living screen,
So close you almost sense them in the play of movement
Glazing off your own form in a shop-front window,

Like the revenants of dogged film noir private eyes
Who shadow their suspect's every move, who ghost
Their oblivious quarry by blending into the crowd.

Over time, they come to regard your every intimacy
Until you're naked as a newborn before the afterlife,
The more so since you still believe you are alone,

That your solitude, even in your happiest moments
Spent with your wife or your remaining friends,
Can be unfurled, the banner of your inmost self,

Even if it's blazoned with the pretentious seal
Of your delusion. Is it their own failures toward you
Summoning them back to the un-resolving world?

Or what Agency do they report to with your foibles,
Mutterings, the wild outbursts of dread and dismay
You thought no one would hear, the unguarded rituals

Performed behind the closed doors they walk through
As if now were the moment they would make your arrest?
Though maybe they're only present like the part of you

That trails your life like a moon on a clear evening,
A new moon burning its absent reflection in a pond,
The light of its full face turned wholly to the other side.

2010

Chin Music

Whenever I look at this photograph
that hangs beside the bookshelf in my study, I sharpen
     my eyes like a batter
who trains on the curveball bending toward the plate,
        trying to judge

  its spin. And like a curve it seems
to defy physics, how these two once occupied the same
     time and space
and still do inside this frame: The Babe[42] as you'd expect
        commanding the center,

  the rest of the hunting party spreading out
the lesser of the tribe around their chief;
     and there, beside him, his hair
slicked back, no longer a wild clownish ring, looking
        the young rabbi:

  Larry,[43] the lowliest stooge, third fiddle
after Moe and Curly, the straight man whose antic pleas
     always seemed more desperate
for having glimpsed the desperate truth. Forget Patroklus;
        think instead of Achilles

  in love with Caliban, or Gilgamesh
roving out for battle beside Polonius. Think of the Stooges
     beside a beefcake Herakles
in a wacky fifties riff on Homeric myth. Or, rather, think
        of Everett Brundage

  who owned the lodge where this photo
was taken—it had to be sometime in the thirties—
     before the Babe's moon-shot drives
arced into legend; before Larry starred with Curly and Moe
        in their madcap parody

---

42 George Herman "Babe" Ruth [1895–1948] was a nearly mythic baseball player.
43 Larry Fine [1902–1975], born Louis Feinberg, was a member of the famous comedy act The Three Stooges.

of Hitler's Germany. I have a tee shirt that reads
"I've seen the future, and it's Fine," where Larry's face
      shrieks in neon
as if he'd shaken hands with a thousand volts, his whole head
         flashing like an absurd Medusa.

    Though when I remember Everett,
I think of a man who for years kept this lodge alive,
      a taxidermist's paradise
of deer heads, antlers, bobcats, and one full-size black bear
         on the fringe of big resorts.

  I remember he had the keenest eyes,
that the whole raucous crowd of locals and exiles
      from the city gathered
at his bar, one manifold tribe roaring on into the night.
         But I remember, too

    those nights he drank until my father
closed the bar and drove him home; how he lived alone
      though he had a wife
who'd left him; how his help—they were friends—stole quietly
         from the till,

    and he lost the lodge, the one thing he loved.
And whenever I remember how they found him sprawled
      dead in the dive
he'd opened on the highway, it makes me think of the phrase
         "Chin music,"

    meaning a high hard one, a tough pitcher's
brush back of the batter who leans too far over the plate.
      "Chin music" was what he said
that afternoon my father drove us down to the lodge
         just before it closed.

On TV the pitcher reared into his wind-up,
and swooping down fired a fastball that started letter high,
            and rose in a perfect
jet stream directly at the batter's head, driving him to the dirt.
            "That's chin music,"

    Everett said, leaning his big body
over the bar, his broad nose and wry grin not unlike the Babe's,
        "it's how life plays you
before you go down for good." Do I have to say he gave me
            the photo for a gift,

    that I'm as awestruck now by its sheer
improbability, having watched those stilted newsreels
            of the great,
the baffled mania of the stooge who took hammer blows to his head,
            who had his eyes

    poked out, it seemed, a thousand times?—
the stooges, with their own chin music, that made me think
        there was no pain.
In the photograph the turkey splays its feathers before the hunters,
            one a hero,

    one a thoughtful man who played the fool.
Did Everett take this picture, thrilled to have fame and greatness
        come to this unlikely place?
The crowd fans out, mostly smiling, around the kill: Who are
            all these nameless men?

                        2008

Where Late the Sweet Birds[44]

As though I'd summoned it with the word *behold*,
A starling flew from maple leaves that hang
Above my patio, green shade, and summer cold
As fall. A plane flared overhead. Nothing sang.
Jackhammers clanged the heart out of the day
While the sun arced imperceptibly west.
The bird scavenged before it flew away,
Scraps among poly-noses and the rest
Of what spring had rained down: lust's golden fire
To fill the earth with passing. It's no lie,
The wind with its sleight from *aspire* to *expire*,
And the wish I wished as the bird streaked by
Longing, in its dumb way, to make the thing strong—
The nest toward which it flew that will not last long.

2010

An Echo on the Narrows

What are you, Never-to-Be, but my own voice	*Voice,*
returning like light waves from outer space	*space*
while the red-shifting stars accelerate	*accelerate*
beyond eye-shot in the all-freezing distance?	*distance.*
Sometimes I think I see you through dark glass,	*Glass*
plucked into being. And the dream consoles	*consoles*
of infinite strings, of far fields only	*only*
separated like lives beheld at a glance.	*at a glance.*

---

44 This poem plays *bouts-rimés* with Shakespeare's Sonnet 73. Joseph Addison defined *bouts-rimés* as "lists of words that rhyme to one another, drawn up by another hand, and given to a poet, who was to make a poem to the rhymes in the same order that they were placed upon the list." Thus, Tobin's poem uses the same rhyme-words as Shakespeare's Sonnet 73 in the same order used by Shakespeare.

I want the world to whirl at my embrace;   *Brace*
or better, you are beside a shore yourself,   *yourself.*
your small hands reaching—though the winds are stiff—   *Stiff*
prizing shells between the foam and currents.   *currents*

And I angle my lens for light to hold   *hold*
you in its sight until I am no one.   *no one.*

—*for a son not born*

2014

Homage to Bosch[45]

All flesh is grass, and all goodliness thereof is the flower of the field.
—Isaiah 40:6

And it was done. The universe a clear ball
gathering dust on nothing's highest shelf,
its snows drifted to mists from which the earth
rises, *en grisaille*,[46] to its first morning.
Rivers and valleys. Rolling hills. Mountains
quickened from the ash of their vanishing.
A landscape colorless, before memory,
pierced by a ray from the receding whirlwind.
Above, sad-faced, ringed by clouds, God opens
his *Summa*, book of judgment and of straw.

I.

Our procession filed through the opened gates
         of the Prado, leaving behind
the guitarists, sword-sellers, bronze horsemen
         of Madrid. Forty schoolboys,

---

45 Hieronymus Bosch [1450–1516]: a Dutch master-painter.
46 "en grisaille": a term from painting denoting works rendered entirely in shades of gray.

faces daubed with acne, what did we know
        about the provinces of art?
We'd have preferred the hotel pool, tapestries
        of beachtowels, bikinis,
bold impastos of the Ramblas, Torremolinos.
        Through rooms of portraits, scions
of history, I shadowed like the town fool
        who stumbles into a coronation.
Then, more fabulous than a roadside carnival:
        The Garden of Earthly Delights—
swarms of nudes, drunk on the juice of berries
        bigger than balloons, tumbling
in the soft grass among seeds of pomegranates,
        enormous fish, shimmering
bubbles housing lovers, kingfishers, goldfinches
        parading toward the cavalcade
(a bestiary turning back on itself like a serpent
        eating its own tail) circling
the central pool. Was this sin or innocence,
        to skinny-dip with dragonflies,
paddle downstream in an apple-boat, or don the head
        of an owl to dance flamenco?
The thirteen-year-old I was woke to the choices:
        On the left wing, the Garden,
Christ in the gesture of a healer taking Eve's hand,
        Adam looking on, his feet
touching the divine gown while behind them the Fountain
        of Life pours out its rivers.
And on the right, the furnace-city of Hell,
        like a photograph of Dresden;
musicians crucified on harps, an enthroned demon
        with a chamber pot crown
defecating the damned into torment's cesspool.
        Only now, years later, do I see
in the background of Paradise that lion rending
        the carcass of a deer,
how it's mirrored in the monster who's turned
        into a macabre Tree of Knowledge,

the sharp limbs piercing the cracked eggshell of skin
        in which devils sit at table—
as if evil had fashioned a tavern in the guts. . . .
        That summer drifts, *sfumato*,[47]
in the haze of memory: the Prado, Toledo,
        Ávila, Montserrat, a man
collared by soldiers on the line to Gibraltar,
        beaten senseless, dragged off.

II.

How plentiful the world is, a wagon piled to bursting
   with its golden trove of hay, wheels wobbling
   underneath, squeaking, the great load teetering
   in every rut.

We parade it through harvest fields, imagining before us
   towns untouched by plague, abuzz with a babble of markets,
   revels uninspired by the feast days of saints—
   a kingdom of our own.

For us, every day is Mardi Gras. We crowd the driven cart
   in scarlet tunics, emerald buskins, royal robes,
   pale turbans, homespun wools, muslins and silks
   as we whirl ahead in our St. Vitus Dance.

We trundle like an army through leveled forests once rife
   with deer, wild boar, the ghosts of extinct species,
   while behind us lands spread out in shimmering haze
   as on the third day of creation.

Lords, emperors, archbishops, kings, their pockets heavy
   with the weight of tithes; knights mantled in armor
   speckled with the blood of crusades; ruminant clerics,
   all train in back, marking their lots like destiny.

---

47 "Sfumato": the painterly technique of allowing colors to blend together gradually in order to create a hazy appearance.

Where a jigging burgher clutches his purse to his heart,
   another pitches his ladder to the wain, hoping to climb
   atop to where a courtier with lute serenades a maid.

Do they hear the song below, those tearing at the stack,
   tearing at each other as they're crushed
   beneath the wheels?

The feasters turn away, sweet smells exuding
   from the campground—a pig's head roasting on its spit,
   trout on poles awaiting flame, casks of wine. . . .

Still we progress in our exodus, riotous as the rabble
   who fashioned a golden calf.

And what if, human, we were blinded by such fullness,
   cajoled by subaqueous demons who would brandish our heads
   on pikes—who's to say our fate could be otherwise?

The saint crouches in reverence over his testament, prey
   for spirits who taunt him from an altar spread
   with bread and wine.

Or from the hollowed trunk of an oak the temptress calls
   his name, fingering herself, while flying fish,
   bird-boats, ascend infernal skies.

The sufferings of the damned and saved, how alike they are—
   as if the Almighty sharpened his blade for all equally,
   and the arms extended in universal blessing
   were only the austere gesture of some bitter judgment.

And so that faint glow on the horizon must be Utopia,
   earthly paradise, the torchlights of the millennium
   and final consummation burning in the eyes of a thief
   who slits his brother's throat for a fistful of straw.

III.

In Carpentras[48] the dead are rising,
           joined by angels,
stunned to ecstasy by the beneficence
           of light that lifts them
into its tunnel, a blinding cornucopia.
           Assumed, do they forget
the desecration of their bodies?
           Or have they accomplished
in their passing what we cannot:
           forgiveness,
even of unimaginable horror?
           I cling to my wrongs—
how as a child I couldn't pull the wings
           off butterflies
at others' egging, but secretly wished
           for the deaths
of those boys who'd surround me
           after school, faces
turned into a canvas of leering masks;
           or my own betrayals—
the friends outgrown, lovers left,
           family denied.
Puffed as Midas who fingered all he saw
           into gold,
I acclaim my ambition to exceed
           and call it virtue,
the way a dandy admires his image
           in a mirror.
Is this, then, goodness: the arm of a boy
           suddenly gone limp
when, charged by hurt, he most desires
           to strike?
Is that why so often the world appears
           unbearable,

---

48 "Carpentras": a Roman Catholic diocese in Provence up until 1801.

because what is most truly us—the part
      that suffers—
can't free itself from the cramped room
      we've furnished for it
in the remotest mansion of ourselves?
      In that barn,
the bewildered child accepts the gifts
      of this world,
while behind him on the torn plain
      crazed horsemen clash.
Too soon he'll wake to the nightmare
      of mocking faces
that crowd him till his own is obscured
      in the rush of torture,
the driven cross. . . . I bear on my back
      the weight of my own skin.

Bones on the road. A wreckage of weapons.
In clear light killers tie their victim
to a tree as another man hunkers off,
abandoned to his dream of refuge.
There are lovers in the meadows, pipers
in fields. And on a far hill a throng
gathers for an execution. Through this land
the wanderer passes, his staff edging back
a rabid dog. . . . Empty One, Unnamable,
only by your command are we sustained.

2004

AFTERMATH
(9/11/01)

It will not be
how the saint imagined,

the soul distilling
into what comes after

the way a woman
wades into ocean

that laps her skin
at body temperature

so she feels herself
the waves' completion,

a fluency
of wine in water,

her body all flow
as she slides under

then out of herself
like a silk nightgown

though you wish it so,
though you wish it so.

Instead, these ashes
through the flood-lit night,

through the silent heaven,
rising, rising. . . .

2005

James Matthew Wilson (1975)

James Matthew Wilson was born in East Lansing, Michigan. He graduated from the University of Michigan in 1998 with a BA in English and Creative Writing. He received an MA from the University of Massachusetts-Amherst (2001), before receiving an MFA (2005) and a PhD (2006) from the University of Notre Dame.

As the late Helen Pinkerton Trimpi writes, "James Matthew Wilson's poems are those of a searching, philosophical, and subtle mind treating themes of the inner and outer life of our contemporary world." Though they are certainly "searching, philosophical, and subtle," Wilson's poems avoid the recherché by deploying language with a kind of hard clarity reminiscent of Yvor Winters's work. In fact, Wilson's poems sometimes assume a public voice generally associated with poets of a bygone age, such as Henry Wadsworth Longfellow. As Dana Gioia has noted, Wilson's is "not the music of the humble shepherd's pipe but the double keyboard pipe organ—resonant, complex, and contrapuntal." In 2019 Wilson published *The River of the Immaculate Conception*, a long sequence responding at once to Frank LaRocca's composition *The Mass of the Americas* and to Hart Crane's *The Bridge*. On the other hand, he is also capable of a sustained psychological exploration of dissipation, as in his 2018 sonnet sequence, "Wiped Out." In short, his content is various, as are his forms, though Wilson's best poems sing out, as Frederick Turner notes, with "a prophetic bluntness that breaks our expectations and makes them gash gold vermilion."

Wilson's work appears in periodicals such as *Best American Poetry*, *First Things*, *The Hopkins Review*, *The Hudson Review*, *Literary Matters*, and *The New Criterion*. He has been awarded various distinctions by the Conference on Christianity and Literature, the Catholic Press Association, *America* magazine, and *Dappled Things*, and he was the winner of the prestigious Hiett Prize in the Humanities in 2017. He teaches at the University of Saint Thomas, Houston, where he co-founded the Master of Fine Arts program. Poet-in-Residence for the Benedict XVI Institute for Sacred Music and Divine Worship, he also is Poetry Editor at *Modern Age*.

Bibliography
Poems: *Some Permanent Things* (2014); *The Hanging God* (2018); *The River of the Immaculate Conception* (2019); *The Strangeness of the Good* (2020); *Saint Thomas and the Forbidden Birds* (2024). Criticism: *The Catholic Imagination in Modern American Poetry* (2014); *The Fortunes of Poetry in an Age of Unmaking* (2015); *The Vision of the Soul: Truth, Goodness and Beauty In the Western Tradition* (2017); *Catholic Modernism and the Irish "Avant Garde": The Achievement of Brian Coffey, Denis Devlin, and Thomas MacGreevy* (2023); *T.S. Eliot: Culture and Anarchy* (2024).

SEE

See, from the hall, the sad men sit,
    The television on, but their
Eyes turned from it,
    Left aching for an answering stare.

See, how the soft boots of this girl
    Shuffle so slowly down the stairs,
Lost in a whirl
    Of cold slights and cosmetic cares.

See, too, the light of evening rake
    The clouds that roll across the sky
And do not break,
    But silent, threatening, pass us by.

And see, and see, into the dark,
    Where spoiled wants and words ferment;
Or that strange park
    Where guilt still loiters, old and bent.

Our bodies harbor the abyss
    On whose source we all speculate:
What is its wish
    That whips our longing, goads our hate?

That leaves us glowering over its deep,
    Discerning shadow within shade,
In which we'd leap
    If that were the sole price we paid?

2018

"Madre de Gracia"[49]

Sunlight flows through St. Mary's windowed corners
With such a grace it seems that all commune
In brilliance, and every surface serves
   Only to magnify with its reflection
   The holy self-expression of the One.

And, in this light-filled place, the cellists tune
As if sweet union's what the world deserves;
And beauty's never beat down by its scorners;
   A vain thought never warped our first affection
   Or concrete weighed the hillsides ton by ton.

Such possibility the introit preserves
With its notes raised for brides as well as mourners,
Remembering and transcending that dark noon,
   Where Judas hanged himself for his defection
   And all the rest stared on a dying son.

2019

On a Palm

The local psychic closed up shop last week;
Took down her shingle with its big black palm
Held up to lure those driving by away
From busy motions to her inner calm;
To draw them where sharp incense burned and scarves
Billowed mysterious shadows down the hall;
Where faded posters of the astral signs
And chakra nodes sagged from each hapless wall.

---

49 This poem, excerpted from *The River of the Immaculate Conception*, responds to the introit of Frank LaRocca's new musical setting of the Catholic Mass, *The Mass of the Americas*, as performed upon its debut in December of 2018 at The Cathedral of Saint Mary of the Assumption in San Francisco, California.

She'd greet them in her gold-ringed gypsy getup,
Her hands emerging to enfold their own
And lead them to a table draped in silks
While querying in a warm and foreign tone.
Of late, she'd clutch them with a tighter grip
And seek to stretch one hour into two
With natal charts, then tarot cards, and listening
For any dead who might be passing through.

I'm glad the window's dark, For Rent sign hung.
But, when I see my hands gripped round the wheel,
The knuckles growing cracked and lined with age,
I think how there is no one who will peel
Them open, lay the fingers gently straight,
And study all those traceries of fate.

2018

A Prayer for Livia Grace

There's little room left in this house for poetry,
Or in this world for any lasting language.
The managers and sales reps in the office
Who've ticketed their holidays are childless,
And looking toward five days of sun and liquor.
They care for neither old books nor a young daughter.

But somehow near me sleeps an infant daughter
Who grows still to the cradle sounds of poetry,
Eyelids dropped in the promise of sleep's liquor.
It charms her, yet she knows nothing of language;
Nor did I, in a way, when I was childless,
Preoccupied with filling another office

Than fatherhood. Now crowded in my office,
A crib and chest of pink drawers for my daughter
Remind me that this empty room sat childless
Except for those ink-littered sheets of poetry,
When "child" was just a word and my child language,
Which I would write and read at night with liquor.

Now she's born, we have little time for liquor,
My desk's crammed in a corner of the office,
And papers lost beneath the brighter language
Of cardboard colored alphabets for my daughter.
I'm sure I wrote a different kind of poetry
When all my hours were filled though I was childless.

The TV news shows that, because they're childless,
Exercise, and shun cigarettes and liquor,
Modern consumers live a life of poetry:
Controlled and self-absorbed as fits the office
Of sonnets or sestinas; their only daughter
An *iPod* or such ephemeral techno-language.

I pray, my daughter, speak another language,
That in the richest sense you not be childless,
Your every act a kind of lasting daughter
More beautiful than bored clerks at their liquor.
Though they find no room for it at the office,
May you crowd your small corridors with poetry.

My daughter's teething, needs her gums rubbed with liquor,
Which stops my language, calls me from my office.
I go. May I have more of this child, less poetry.

2014

MARCH 25, 2020

I thought that looking back upon this time,
I'd view it as the winter without snow.
Out for a walk the other day, I heard
The steady roar of a snowblower running,
Its owner burning off the tank of gas
He'd filled, in late November, when a trace
Of flurries made its feigning fall toward earth.
We do not always read the hour rightly;
The signs the times bear with them are obscured
As if by gusting snow squalls in the headlights.
   And now, it's something else that falls. The virus
Is spreading through New York. A friend of mine,
Holed up in his apartment in Manhattan,
Sends photos out of cans of beans and franks,
Beef chili, paired with bottles of cheap wine
And *Gawain* in a tattered paperback,
All captioned with quotations from Defoe,
And laughing at the way he's been marooned.
   A decade back, I recollect, we shared
Bottles of Yellow Tail at a reception,
And talked of Auden late into the night.
We met the morning after, our heads pounding,
Just like Sir Gawain, knelt in winter snow,
Who waited for the Green Knight's falling axe
That, with one swoop, both spared and chastened him.
   The fearful flee that city like a flood;
The wealthy spilling out into the Hamptons,
Where all the year-round residents, who pour
The drinks and scoop the ice cream through the summer,
Are saying, now, don't come, we cannot take you.
They've covered up the welcome signs, would raise
The bridges if they could, the hospitals
All full, the groceries emptied, far as Montauk.
   I was supposed to catch a New York train
Today myself, but that, of course, is cancelled.

And so, I sat, this morning, on the couch
And read my boys the opening of *Five
Children and It*. Dear Panther and her siblings
Have fled the pestilential streets of London,
Where things are labeled with invisible signs—
Keep Out, or *Do Not Touch*, or *Go Away*—
And every bit of fun gets one in trouble.
They find themselves left at a country house,
Much like the Hamptons, if not quite so nice,
Its chief appeal a neighboring gravel pit.

    While digging to Australia, one day,
Their errant spade turns up a Psammead,
Who startles with his gruff voice, snail-like eyes,
And furry little body snug in sand.
They little know that he will grant them wishes:
Such useless guineas men stare at like sores,
Or giant wings with which to beat the air
And rob a farmer's plum trees of their fruit,
As if avenging angels sent by God.

    James blasts his trumpet in the living room;
The straining pip-pip-pip of reveille
Flies unobstructed through my office door.
It is—oh, yes—Annunciation Day.
How little we expect the news we hear,
Until it comes upon us, brilliant, blazing,
Commanding we not feel the fear we feel,
And that we must unlearn all that we know,
So as to see the hour with new eyes,
And, what is more, to trust, somehow, we will
Endure that fate whose stroke has yet to fall.

2020

APRIL 15, 2020

The children whirl in circles round me there,
Axis and father of them all, their bikes
Humming against cold air, the flash of wheels
Ripping about the empty parking lot
Outside the shuttered public library.
   The only person who intrudes upon
Their endless, free procession: one old man
Who comes each day and plugs his laptop in
With an extension cord, its long orange line
Led snake-like to an outlet in the stone.
He sits there, in his car's back seat, a door
Cracked to admit the power, his white head
Ignoring us and bent in concentration,
As if pure thought turned in upon itself.
   But he should see how those kids whip their way
In narrow, then in greater, orbits flying,
As do the hosts of feathered seraphim,
Formed rank on rank, enclosed in brilliant wings,
And giving of the plenitude they circle,
From greater to the lesser, so that all
Share in the splendor of the sourceless font,
That boundless wheel of light which kindles all.
Such ecstasy and glory have they found
In their but recently acquired balance;
They coast within a haze of radiance.
   Beyond us, stretch the baseball fields, their backstops
Heavy and dull with chain-linked uselessness,
The infields scribbled through with dirt bike tracks.
And, just along the margin of the wood,
The playground we have named for Narnia
Sits idle, swings and jungle gym both wrapped
In orange police tape, snapping back and forth,
Caught in the fitful gusts of April wind.

Just out of sight, still other circles narrow.
The nesting of a man into his lounger,
A case of Lite spread open like a mouth
Beside the leg rest handle. On the set,
An episode recorded some years back
Shows someone spin the wheel or buy an "O."

A woman, frail and shrunken in her blouse,
Has freshened up her tight perm with a pick,
But let it drop back gently on the couch,
Her breath grown shallow, slowed as sleep descends.
And, in the early morning, fathers pace
With bloodshot, angry eyes, the children yelling
And crowding one another at the sink.
The basin's thick with aqua streaks of paste
That cling beneath the cold gush jetting downward.

And somewhere, someone's mother chips a nail
Trying to clean the juice and crumbs that hide
Within the wrinkled padding of a highchair;
And someone locked inside a studio
Whose heart is racing, racing with the boredom
Reels eyes from phone to book to alley window;
While in the paper, blotches pullulate
And overlap upon a printed map
Like an old stack of tiddlywinks we've scattered.

Our dogwoods now stand prim with pinkish flowers,
The maple in the side yard, bulging clusters,
While apple and magnolia shed last petals
In skirts that radiate about their trunks.

Yet, even now, the season's gripped with chill,
And I find, twisting on the air, a few
Stray flurries wend their pointless journey down,
As if to warn us, all that comes to pass
Will be turned back upon itself, in time,
However much time seems one long, straight line.
And, in this spiraling about an axis,
We may see fate, but fate has its own order;
And order brings with it a kind of freedom,
As Thomas proves, when he repeats each arc

About the lot, as if it were the cosmos—
That place of churning planets, winding stars,
And singing angels covering their eyes—
His cycle racing wild its spinning pageant
So fast I hardly note the trepidations.

2020

Ryan Wilson (1982)

Ryan Wilson was born in Griffin, Georgia, and raised in nearby Macon. He received a bachelor's degree in English from the University of Georgia in 2004, an MFA from Johns Hopkins University in 2007, and a second master's degree from Boston University in 2008. His first book, *The Stranger World*, won the Donald Justice Prize for Poetry, and his criticism has received the Jacques Maritain Prize (*Dappled Things*) and the Walter Sullivan Prize (*Sewanee Review*).

In *How to Think Like a Poet*, Wilson writes, "The healthy soul, like the gracious host, must welcome every stranger." Wilson's own poems welcome the quotidian and the mythic, the contemporary and the ancient, generally counterpointing formal precision with mysterious content in dynamic juxtapositions that do not resolve dualistic impulses but embody them. Praised by former US Poet Laureate Robert Pinsky for his "mastery of traditional forms" and for his "idiomatic, American blank verse . . . as fluent as that of Robert Frost," Wilson also deploys rarer forms—such as the alliterative hemistichs of Old English, or the Old French *bref double*—as well as nonce forms. His best poems utilize poetic forms not for their own sake, but as vehicles of mood and meaning, and often turn toward the uncanny. As Rosanna Warren has written, "Ryan Wilson is a poet of nightmares," though she adds that his poems show how "a classical flourish can bring us face to face with horror, or with ourselves." Indeed, Wilson's poems tend toward dramatized psychological explorations. Compared by James Matthew Wilson to those of Donne, Herbert, and Robert Lowell, his poems are such "that particular and universal, concrete and abstract, material and spirit, sacred and secular, are always interpenetrating each other."

Wilson's work appears in periodicals such as *Best American Poetry, Five Points, The Hopkins Review, The New Criterion, Quarterly West, The Sewanee Review*, and *The Yale Review*. Currently the editor of *Literary Matters*, Wilson teaches at the Catholic University of America and in the MFA program at the University of St. Thomas-Houston, and lives in Carroll County, Maryland. He is co-editor of this anthology.

Selected Bibliography
The Stranger World (2017); *How to Think Like a Poet* (2019); *Proteus Bound: Selected Translations, 2008-2020* (2021); *In Ghostlight* (2024).

FOR A DOG

You'd wake us up—that shrill, insistent bark
Driving away whatever dreams had fogged
Our vision—and we'd rise in the true dark,

Wondering just what exactly, catalogued
By canine instinct under 'THREAT,' was there,
What jogger, cat, or dog it was that dogged

You from your drowse beside the easy chair
And summoned your yapped pandemonium.
Nine times in ten it was just empty air,

Some ghosted scent you sniffed. Dumb—you were dumb,
Like all dogs, snuffling up to snakes, afraid
Of mice. When we said 'come,' you wouldn't come;

You capered when commanded to play dead,
And when we wanted most to be alone
You'd offer up that imbecilic head

Until we crowned your pity with a bone.
Our lives took on the shape you spun from need,
The harried rondure of routine. You gone,

The house is quieter, and we've been freed
Forever from the never-ending chores
Your tail entailed, the scrubbing where you peed,

The hunting stain-removers down in stores.
What's hardest are the peaceful hours we wanted
So much when you were scratching up the doors

And howling at some phantom thing that haunted
The world without, some threat we couldn't see
That you were desperate to have confronted.

Now you're part of that present unity
Of absences the living move among,
In which what was, what will, and what can't be

Dance in a ring to a triumphant song
We don't have ears to hear, or heart to see,
Who sleep now perfectly, and much too long.

2017

DISOBEDIENCE

Piazza San Marco

Here at the labyrinth's heart, I find the air
Is scintillant, just like the postcards show:
A dream of light and strict geometries.
Where the lagoon's receded from the square
Gray stones are dazzled with a blinding glow,
And crowds wait, wincing, in the shimmer's frieze

Like marble waiting for some word or spell
To conjure limbs to life from lifeless stasis,
Or nomads, stunned to find a sudden well
Amid the endless sands, or an oasis.

I feel it. Nightly angst, ennui, and gloom
Refine the human need for some perfection,
Some otherwhere outside routine's dark delves,
And here we are in 'Europe's drawing room,'
Napoleon's choicest spot. Sun-glare's reflection
In café windows, we can't see ourselves

At all, which is, I guess, why we worked out
Ways to scrounge up the cash, made plans, and took
The flights. We've dreamed the us we've dreamed about
Awaits us here. But no, not here. See, look:

Campanile cracked, Venetians flee *en masse*.
The ones stuck here hawk trinkets. For a coin
Tourists go chattering by St. Mark's bones,
And maybe stop a second, as they pass,
Thinking of their rivals back home in Des Moines,
To snap some well-posed selfies with their phones.

Outside, a blizzard of chivalric white,
The sea-gulls swarm, whirling in clean white air,
And then descend, like jagged shards of light,
To peck to death a pigeon in the square,

Removing flesh until, pink as a tongue,
The innards show. The passersby ignore
The wound, the bird. But there's a girl with bread,
One not too busy being rich or young,
Crouched in the square, small, casting morsels for
The living ones. A saint, I almost said—

It is illegal here to feed a pigeon,
Yet she does, quietly, sure that the law,
Which holds the bottom line's the true religion,
Shall not expunge this world's dark, wingèd flaw.

2024

FACE IT

A silence, bodied like wing-beaten air,
Perturbs your face sometimes when parties end
And, half-drunk, you stand looking at some star
That flickers like a coin wished down a well,
Or when you hear a voice behind you whisper
Your name, and turn around, and no one's there.
You're in it then, once more, the stranger's house

Perched in the mountain woods, the rot-sweet smell
Of Fall, the maples' millions, tongues of fire,
And there, whirl harrowing the gap, squint-far,
That unidentified fleck, approaching and
Receding at once, rapt in the wind's spell—
Pulse, throb, winged dark that haunts the clean light's glare—
That thing that you're becoming, that you are.

2017

PHILOCTETES, LONG AFTERWARD[50]

They're nice to me, I guess,
These ghosts who never quite know what to say,
   Having lived out meaningless
Lives here in Thessaly. They fear each day
   That they have been somehow defrauded,
      But bring me my Dilaudid
Out on this sunny terrace anyway

   In their soft shoes and scrubs.
They putter forward into their futures while
      Helping us into tubs
Or pushing Lethean[51] pills to coax a smile
   From us, who see, played on these plains
      Once more, our ancient pains,
The green a stage that holds Troy's burning pile.

---

50 Philoctetes was an Argive hero from Thessaly. Due to a foul-smelling wound on his foot, he was abandoned on the isle of Lemnos by Odysseus and company *en route* to Troy, and he lived ten years alone in the wilderness before Calchas prophesied the Argives could not win the war without him and the magical bow (which could not miss its target) that he had been given by Heracles prior to that demi-god's death. Upon this prophecy, Odysseus and Pyrrhus, son of the late Achilles, sailed to Lemnos to persuade Philoctetes to rejoin their forces. He resisted their entreaties until, in Sophocles' play named for him, Philoctetes was confronted by Heracles, risen from the dead in a *deus ex machina* that resolves the conflict. He is mentioned briefly in *The Iliad*.
51 Lethe is the river of forgetfulness in Hades, the Classical realm of the dead.

It's like some movie set,
This hospice. We're the actors; they're the crew.
    They bring our Percocet
And coffee, do the lights. What do we do?
    We act like we are still the men
        We were, in that time when
Our lives still mattered. Could be worse. It's true

    Time's poison ravages
The body, but what are gout and diabetes
    To one who knows what he is,
What he was? What can they be to Philoctetes?
    I am the man who slaughtered Paris[52]
        For his crime, here, on a terrace
In a wheelchair, dribbling milk from soggy Wheaties,

    Browbeaten by these ghosts
Who've never lived. Here's the survivor's fate.
    And always with the ghosts. . .
My own dead friend came to equivocate
    For Pyrrhus and Odysseus,
        And he made such a fuss
That I slouched off to fight for men I hate.

    For what? Lo! My reward
For saving the Achaeans with my bow?
    Great Agamemnon, Lord
Of Men, long dead; Achilles, too, laid low,
    And no one cares what they debated
        Or how, manipulated,
I left where Lemnos' sleepy breezes blow

    As soft as Mother Peace
Upon the fevered brow of her sick child,
    Who's sick with the disease
Of life. They could have left me in the wild
    Where I'd hobble from my quiet cave
        Like Lazarus from the grave,
My dying and my living reconciled

---

52 Traditionally, Philoctetes kills Paris Alexandros with his infallible bow and arrow.

As in an afterlife
I could not end, since ending it would mean
   Another afterlife.
I've never seen such darkly brilliant green. . .
  Living on bread the ravens brought
   And the few fish I caught. . .
Things I'd ignored for years took on the sheen

   Of jeweled seas at noon,
The deep-down stir of things made evident
   While I lay in a swoon
On a stone ledge above the forest, bent
  Over a sprig of thyme, white-capped,
   As if some breaker lapped
Within the limestone shelf its growth had rent.

   The changeful days were changeless,
And I was most alive when numbered dead,
   When the unexpected angels
Of daily observation crowned my head
  As mayflies form a halo over
   A lily in the clover
Nobody's ever seen. But now, instead

   Of that, the TV blares,
I e-mail different people. Memory fades.
   We're dying. No one cares.
They feed us burnt steaks. We wield plastic blades,
  And wish we'd known the naïve joy
   Of those love felled at Troy,
Who don't now live as shades among the shades.

2024

Heorot[53]

Nov., 2016

It is creeping across

the withered backcountry.

Where grim fogs graze hills

and gray mists haunt

the hollows that hug

our forsaken highways,

it lurches through thickets,

downs leaves, downs limbs.

It strips the bronze stalks

of the harvest, it steals

the firstling of the flock

to gladden its feeding.

In a ditch by our fence

they found Doc's daughter.

The balefires burn.

Others are butchered.

Groped by our grief,

in the grizzled air

we have shrieked lamentations,

longing for a law

to punish the predator

and make firm a peace.

All the high councils

have condemned the creature,

and still it stands

astride the county,

cruel as winter,

the cold's own kinsman.

The nightly news

repeats its nothing;

our Facebook friends

cry wolf, unfollow us.

---

53 "Heorot" is King Hrothgar's mead-hall in the Anglo-Saxon poem *Beowulf*.

It shakes its iron

        shackles in the shadows,

it rattles its wrench

        over the roof gables,

in the darkness outside

        our doors, it dances,

and will not wander

        from the farms it has wasted,

the monstrous changeling,

        unchosen, our child.

2024

In the Harvest Season

It's finished. Waiting's all that will remain.
That gossip now must go unverified.
Blue smoke from leaf-piles, smoldering like pride,
Hangs here, a ghost, a storm-cloud that can't rain.
Last night, the county's final weathervane
Fell in the high winds. Old roofs, stripped bare, preside.
Take down the ragged self you've crucified
And let the crows wing through the fields of grain.

The sagging fence will never stand up straight.
Whatever's not ripe now will never be.
That pain tormenting you will not abate,
And in the windows of vacated banks
You'll see yourself, passing by aimlessly.
You cannot change your life. Give up; give thanks.

2017

Franz Wright (1953–2015)

Franz Wright was born in Vienna, Austria, where his father, the poet James Wright, was studying on a Fulbright Fellowship; he grew up in Seattle, the Midwest, and the San Francisco Bay Area. Though James Wright left the family when Franz was young, father and son maintained a relationship, frequently a fraught one. Wright earned a BA from Oberlin College in 1977, but during his college years he began to struggle with addiction, a struggle that would, combined with depression, lead to several hospitalizations and to periods of homelessness. After losing a position at Emerson College, Wright found himself at the University of Arkansas, where he met scholar and translator Elizabeth Oehlkers, whose relationship with Wright led him to sobriety, to a conversion to Roman Catholicism, and to the best poems he would ever write. The two were wed in 1999, and Wright's next book, *The Beforelife*, was a finalist for the Pulitzer Prize, while his subsequent volume, *Walking to Martha's Vineyard*, won the Pulitzer Prize in 2004. The recipient of numerous other awards—including a Whiting Award, a Guggenheim Fellowship, two grants from the NEA, and the 1996 PEN / Voelcker Award for Poetry—Wright published in periodicals such as *Best American Poetry, Field, The New Yorker*, and *Poetry*.

The eminent critic Helen Vendler has noted, "Wright's scale of experience, like [John] Berryman's, runs from the homicidal to the ecstatic," and has praised his "startling metaphors, starkness of speech, compression of both pain and joy, and a stoic self-possession within the agonies and penalties of existence." Indeed, his finest poems look unflinchingly at human misery and yet retain a sense of gallows humor, often leading the reader through self-loathing and self-pity toward the light of peace. Influenced by the haunting imagery of Bashō, the Surrealist tendencies of René Char, the lyricism of Rilke, and the fearlessness of Baudelaire, Wright's poems frequently rely on puns, sleights of syntax, and subtle lineation to generate multiple meanings simultaneously, allowing him to chronicle and explore the paradoxes of the human spirit. His poems—typically short and possessing the appearance on the page of fragments—often encounter discoveries in the white space between lines and stanzas, embodying the kind of apophatic theology that led him to write, in the poem "Letter," that "We are created by being destroyed." Wright died of lung cancer in 2015 at his home in Waltham, Massachusetts.

Selected Bibliography
Earlier Poems (2007); *The Beforelife* (2000); *Walking to Martha's Vineyard* (2003); *God's Silence* (2006); *Wheeling Motel* (2009); *Kindertotenwald* (2011); *F* (2013)

Year One

I was still standing
on a northern corner.

Moonlit winter clouds the color of the desperation of wolves.

Proof
of Your existence? There is nothing
but.

2003

Transfusion

Strange, I suffered from none of these symptoms until I was so
intensively treated for them. Now I'm always freezing, and have
evidently been shattered into five or six chattering replications of
myself, all leaning in utter exhaustion on very thin canes made of
glass.

I remember the night we were torn like a page from our sleep:

I, your telephone, command you to report to the ER without delay.

The last thing you see is the first.

This time it seems I woke up with pneumonia, anemia, tuber-
culosis (further tests will be required), crucifixion by toothache, a
shadow by night, &c. Clearly, I will never be the same. Yet you
are with me.

To your entire satisfaction has anyone described the look of love?
Mine neither; but I have seen it.

I'm seeing it right now.

I am traveling up the beams of your eyes. I am slowly being low-
ered into a place of light.

2011

Memoir

Just hope he forgot the address
and don't answer the phone

for a week:
put out all the lights

in the house—
behave like you aren't there

if some night when
it's blizzarding, you see

Franz Wright arrive
on your street with his suitcase

of codeine pills,
lugging that heavy

black manuscript
of blank texts.

2000

BAUDELAIRE[54]

"When I have inspired universal horror
I shall have conquered solitude,"
he wrote in his journal, in his rented misery.

Interesting strategy. The person who wrote
this was an ill and wrathful man. One
who constantly strove to do better, composer

of a couple sad dope-sickness remedies—
Icelandic moss?—and the firm resolution
to pray every morning to God, his mother

and Edgar Allan Poe. Who made,
the splendid mind, to self, this note:
"Whenever you receive a letter from a creditor

immediately write fifty lines
upon an otherworldly subject,
and you will be saved!" (If not from the stepfool.)

His throne a wheelchair in an empty park;
the satanic baby, *enfant du mal*, and Mom
the true power behind it right to the end.

Evil isn't hard to comprehend, it is nothing
but unhappiness
in its most successful disguise.

Evil is hated and feared at least.
It is possessed, unlike mere misery,
of a dark glamour nobody pities.

2009

---

54 Charles Baudelaire [1821–1867]: widely regarded as the greatest French poet of the nineteenth century.

LETTER
January 1998

I am not acquainted with anyone
there, if they spoke to me
I would not know what to do.
But so far nobody has, I know
I certainly wouldn't.
I don't participate, I'm not allowed;
I just listen, and every morning
have a moment of such happiness, I breathe
and breathe until the terror returns. About the time
when they are supposed to greet one another
two people actually look into each other's eyes
and hold hands a moment, but
the church is so big and the few who are there
are seated far apart. So this presents no real problem.
I keep my eyes fixed on the great naked corpse, the vertical corpse
who is said to be love
and who spoke the world
into being, before coming here
to be tortured and executed by it.
I don't know what I am doing there. I do
notice the more I lose touch
with what I previously saw as my life
the more real my spot in the dark winter pew becomes—
it is infinite. What we experience
as space, the sky
that is, the sun, the stars
is intimate and rather small by comparison.
When I step outside the ugliness is so shattering
it has become dear to me, like a retarded
child, precious to me.
If only I could tell someone.
The humiliation I go through
when I think of my past
can only be described as grace.
We are created by being destroyed.

2003

P.S.

I close my eyes and see
a seagull in the desert,
high, against unbearably blue sky.

There is hope in the past.

I'm writing to you
all the time, I am writing

with both hands,
day and night.

2003

Crumpled-Up Note Blowing Away

Were no one
here to witness it,
could the sun be
said to shine? Clearly,
you pedantic fool.

But I've said all that
I had to say.
In writing.
I signed my name.
It's death's move.

It can have mine, too.
It's a perfect June morning,
and I just turned eighteen;
I can't even believe
what I feel like today.

Here am I, Lord,
sitting on a suitcase,
waiting for my train.
The sun is shining.
I'm never coming back.

2013

David Yezzi (1966)

David Yezzi was born in 1966 in Albany, New York. He received a bachelor's degree in Theater from Carnegie-Mellon University and an MFA from Columbia University before attending Stanford University as a Stegner Fellow from 1998–2000. A former director of the Unterberg Poetry Center of the 92nd Street Y (2001–2005) and former executive editor of *The New Criterion*, he has also served as chair of the Writing Seminars at Johns Hopkins University and as editor of *The Hopkins Review*. The author of five full-length collections of poems, Yezzi regularly publishes poems and critical prose in leading periodicals such as *The Atlantic, Best American Poetry, The New York Times, The Paris Review, Poetry, The Wall Street Journal,* and *The Yale Review*.

Praised by Harold Bloom for their "severe grace and elegiac intensity," Yezzi's poems often begin with the domestic and move, via dramatic vocal modulations, toward discovery. In fact, Yezzi is not only one of the very best American poets and editors of his generation, but he is also a fine playwright—as well as an incisive and influential critic. His background in the theater informs the dramatic movement of his lyrics, which often blend contemporary slang and the vernacular with psychological or philosophical meditation in a manner reminiscent of the School of Donne, though this sophisticated blend is, to some degree, masked by a colloquial quality that recalls the "plain style" of Ben Jonson. Alternating between vigorous linguistic compression and seemingly casual utterances, Yezzi's poems are equally hospitable to Shakespeare or to the rock star Prince, to Ovid or to Instagram.

Indeed, as Anthony Hecht has written, Yezzi's poetry is "wonderfully versatile." Adept in both open forms and in the most rigorous of traditional forms, Yezzi is—like Hecht, whose authorized biography he has written—a poet of understatement and subtlety, irony and peripeteia, wit and a masterful grace of movement.

Selected Bibliography

Poems: *The Hidden Model* (2003); *Azores* (2008); *Birds of the Air* (2013); *Black Sea* (2018); *Schnauzer: A Play in One Act* (2018); *More Things in Heaven: New and Selected Poems* (2022); as editor, *The Swallow Anthology of New American Poets* (Swallow Press, 2009); as biographer, *Late Romance: Anthony Hecht—A Poet's Life* (2023).

CRANE

Paper creased is
with a touch
made less by half,
reduced as much

again by a second
fold—so the wish
to press our designs
can diminish

what we hold.
But by your hand's
careful work,
I understand

how this unleaving
makes of what's before
something finer
and finally more.

2013

TYGER, TYGER

They went to an abandoned home to smoke weed. Inside, they found a tiger.
—CNN

Strong bud. Mind-splitting, hydroponic, pure indica body-high, one-hit weed,
grown from Hawaiian seeds in a closet in a doublewide in Maine, up near
     Canada.

To say it unleashed the tiger is to say everything and nothing. To say that they
     had
failed to foresee the consequences of their actions is to be complicitly young.

Eve had the weed and Adam had the papers. And they'd been having sex, in
   fields
and organ lofts and in abandoned houses. Even so, you never forget your first
   tiger.

Nor had they dreamed it, like the Argentine writer Julio Cortázar, who
   imagined
how it might be possible to share a living space with a wild creature, or, more

to the point how it would *not* be possible. What if the tiger claimed more and
   more
space until the house was split in half? The parlors and the dining room

and the foyer and the stairs would become the tiger's, and the rest under threat,
cramped and, because the thermostat was in the half gone out of bounds, cold.

So here they were: the boy and the girl. And the weed, though they hadn't
even gotten around to smoking it, when this sleek shimmer and ripple

of muscle entered the room. At first they were not afraid of it; rather they
fully expected that, wherever they went, extraordinary things would follow
   them,

and if that took the form of an emerald-eyed carnivore with a voice like a fault
   line,
then this was only different in degree and not in kind from what they had come

to feel was the new normal of their time together, both high and sober, either
in public, at the movies, under the Milky Way, in the bushes, or in the dark

secret confines of a house where no one had lived for years except a tiger.
There was nothing really strange about it, only that they began to fear for its

care over time: sweeping out the rooms, arranging for food and medicine
should the tiger fall ill with a viral infection or suppuration from an ingrown
   claw.

But wasn't it their tiger? They had found it. My tiger is your tiger, she had told
 him.
"Finding a forever home for a tiger is not easy," said the game warden, who took

the tiger in, bathed it and kept it in a cage, for future transfer to a willing zoo,
where its movements would be remarked on, the way that memories are,

at a distance, through wrought-iron bars, the tiger growing listless, eyes dimmed
except on those occasions when a pair of stoned kids, holding hands and
 pausing

before him, gaze in and recognize something familiar, and, full of mischief
and impunity, guided by a sense of natural law, whisper a secret plan to set it
 free.

2022

The Chain

Outside Giant[55]
a woman, whose child—
one of three, all under ten,
and this one maybe five,
 a girl—is going wild,
crying (keening really),
up the canned goods aisle,
 past the Wonder,
 crazed, noncompliant,
 face borscht red,

 now breaks down
 herself—the mom, I mean—
grabbing the kid by the coat.

---

55 A chain of grocery stores.

She pulls her close and screams
  something PG-13
in the half-full parking lot,
not caring that we've seen
  her lose her shit.
     Two cars down,
  a guy, foot-lit

    by tail lights,
  starts tsking as he pops his trunk,
saying good and loud, for me to hear,
"That's no way to treat your kid."
  He wobbles like he's drunk
or has bad hips, slides
into his piece of junk
  and turns it over.
     His brights
  illuminate the river

    of rain
  bubbling like sea spray
across the pocked anchorage
in which our cars are moored.
  On my way
home, it's still needling me:
What's with that guy? Okay,
  he has no children. But who's
    more insane?
He's sure it's her; I choose

    him. And me?
  Tonight my son
actually flinches as he turns
the corner, still stinging from my swat,
  with his Nerf gun
cocked. He paints the enemy,
remembering him red-faced, gone
  ballistic, flashing teeth.
    Down his sights, he
  squints and aims at me.

And I agree:
they will be in his mind
forever, the image of me raging
and the look on his mother's face.
Will he, in his turn, find
a different way to be? So far,
he is, in his finer moments, kind.
Other times he'll turn
raw, like me, and like me
will not learn.

2018

The Good News

A friend calls, so I ask him to stop by.
We sip old Scotch, the good stuff, order in,
some Indian—no frills too fine for him
or me, particularly since it's been
ages since we made the time.

Two drinks in, we've caught up on our plans.
I've sleepwalked through the last few years by rote;
he's had a nasty rough patch, quote-unquote,
on the home front. So, we commiserate,
cupping our lowballs in our hands.

It's great to see him, good to have a friend
who feels the same as you about his lot—
that, while some grass is greener, your small plot
is crudely arable, and though you're not
so young, it's still not quite the end.

As if remembering then, he spills his news.
Though I was pretty lit, I swear it's true,
it was as if a gold glow filled the room
and shone on him, a sun-shaft piercing through
   dense clouds, behind which swept long views.

In that rich light, he looked, not like my friend,
but some acquaintance brushed by on the train.
Had his good fortune kept me from the same,
I had to wonder, a zero-sum game
   that gave the night its early end?

Nothing strange. Our drinks were done, that's all.
We haven't spoken since. By morning, I
couldn't remember half of what the guy
had said, just his good news, my slurred good-bye,
   the click of the latch, the quiet hall.

    2008

FREE PERIOD

   Outside study hall,
it's me, my girlfriend, and a guy
named Rob—bony kid, klutzy
at games, fluent in French.
   He's behind her;

   I'm asleep or half-
asleep (it's morning), and, as I
squint into the trapezoid of light
breaking on the bench and me,
   I see him raise

   his hand to her head
from the back, so gently
she doesn't notice
him at first, but stands there,
   carved in ebony

and beaten gold:
Stacey's straight black hair
falling in shafts of sun.
He smoothes it down,
  firmly now,

  so that she turns,
kind of freaked, as if to say,
"Can you believe it?"
to me still coming to.
   Yes, I guess I can,

  I think to myself,
with only a twinge
of jealousy, with admiration,
actually. And pity—since he'd seen
  beauty raw,

  for which humiliation
was the smallest price,
and, dazzled, grasped at it,
not getting hold.
  It wasn't his, god knows,

  or mine, as I,
months later, learned
hopelessly—almost fatally,
it felt—or even hers, though it was
  of her and around her,

  in that freeze-frame
of low sunshine,
with us irremediably young
and strung-out from love
  and lack of love.

   2013

MINDING RITES

This guy I know, a rabbi, Friday nights
on his way home before sunset in winter,
always stops at a florist or bodega
and buys a bunch of flowers for his wife.

Every week the same, a ritual,
regardless of her mood that morning, fresh
upsets at work, or snarling on the bridge;
he brings her roses wrapped in cellophane.

But isn't there a ring of hokiness
in that? Why should a good man have to show
his devotion? Some things go unspoken;
some things get tested on the real world,

and isn't that the place that matters most?
So when you told me I should bring you flowers,
I joked, "But don't I show my feelings more
in dog walks, diapers, and rewiring lamps?"

The flowers, I learned later, weren't for wooing,
not for affection in long marriage, but
for something seeded even deeper down,
through frost heaves, and which might be, roughly, peace.

(It's funny that I just assumed romance.)
Now there's no peace with us, I wonder what
they might have meant to you, those simple tokens,
holding in sight what no rite can grow back.

2013

WEEDS

My emerald legions, how tall you have grown:
so many. With what supernatural speed

you overlord the weakest in the garden—
frizzled hydrangeas, sere mint, sun-starved basil.

Tousle-headed, you can see the sky
above the cowering, defeated plots.

This is your day of triumph: eager sugars
rise up through your ramifying stalks.

And I allowed it. My cool inattention
found good reasons to look the other way,

since all that grows is good, or so I thought.
How soon would height recall high thoughts, and yet,

if I uproot you now, how I would miss you.
Sweet knotgrass, heartsick briar, purple thistle.

Even tilled up, the garden wouldn't look
as it did when my grandmother warned me

not to grow too fast. She lived to be
a hundred, girlhood lost except for this:

a vague lightness coming, as though of wings
lifting her above the loamy soil,

and all she thought of, as the wind upheld her,
was the packed ground, how tenuous her flight.

Or so I imagine. Though half her age,
I, too, can't quite remember what it felt like

to be light-footed, open to the sun,
without the clogging stems elbowing out

what I meant when I first planted here:
larkspur, geraniums, cilantro, lime.

2018

MOTHER CAREY'S HEN[56]

There are days I don't think about the sea;
   weeks wash by, in fact,
then a shearwater—or some such—flutters by
on the salt flats fanning out in my mind's eye,
reflected there, a shimmering reverie,
       recalling the pact

I once made (and renew today) to hold
   to a higher altitude.
But not the difference between this bird
and me: a slight disruption or harsh word
and I crash, folded seaward, letting cold
       life intrude;

whereas the petrel, mindless of such height,
   scales each watery hill
that rises up, adapting to the shape
of each impediment, each low escape
instinct in it, the scope of its flight
       fitted to its will.

2008

---

56 A seafarer's nickname for the European storm petrel.

ACKNOWLEDGMENTS

We are grateful to the poets and presses for permission to reprint the following poems:

Julia Alvarez, "How I Learned to Sweep," "Folding My Clothes," and "Spic" from *Homecoming*. Copyright © 1984, 1996 by Julia Alvarez. Used by permission of Susan Bergholz Literary Services. "Bilingual Sestina" from *The Other Side/ El Otro Lado*. Copyright © 1995 by Julia Alvarez. Used by permission of Susan Bergholz Literary Services.

Ned Balbo, "Son of Frankenstein" and "Hart Island" from *The Trials of Edgar Allen Poe and Other Poems*. Copyright © 2010 by Ned Balbo. Reprinted with the permission of The Permissions Company, LLC on behalf of Story Line Press, an imprint of Red Hen Press, redhen.org. "Miraculous Spirals" from *Literary Matters*, Winter 2020. Used by permission of *Literary Matters*.

Molly McCully Brown, "The Central Virginia Training Center," "Labor," "Prayer for the Wretched Among Us," and "The Convulsions Choir" from *The Virginia State Colony for Epileptics and Feebleminded*. Copyright © 2017 by Molly McCully Brown. Reprinted by permission of Persea Books, Inc (New York), www.perseabooks.com. All rights reserved.

Maryann Corbett, "Prophesying to the Breath" from *Mid Evil*. Copyright © 2013 by Mary Ann Corbett. Reprinted by permission of University of Evansville Press. "Northeast Digs Out from Record Snowfall" and "Airheads" from *Credo for the Checkout Line in Winter*. Copyright © 2013 by Mary Ann Corbett. Used by permission of Able Muse Press. "Historic District, Walking Garden Tour," "Defending Veronese," and "Staging Directions" from *Street View*. Copyright 2013 by Mary Ann Corbett. Used by permission of Able Muse Press.

Sarah Cortez, "Lingo," "*Tu Negrito*," "A Certain Kind of Case," "Rosie Working Plain Clothes" from *How to Undress a Cop*. Copyright © 2000 by Sarah Cortez. Used by permission of Arte Publico Press.

Kate Daniels, "The Playhouse" from *The White Wave* by Kate Daniels, © 1984. Reprinted by permission of the University of Pittsburgh Press. "Dogtown, 1957" and "Late Apology to Doris Haskins" from *A Walk in Victoria's Secret*. Copyright © 2010 by Kate Daniels. Used by permission of Louisiana State University Press. "Getting Clean" and "Reading a Biography of Thomas Jefferson in the Months of My Son's Recovery" from *In the Months of My Son's Recovery*. Copyright © 2019 by Kate Daniels. Used by permission of Louisiana State University Press. "Niobe of the Painting" and "War Photograph" from *The Niobe Poems* by Kate Daniels, © 1988. Reprinted by permission of the University of Pittsburgh Press. "Prayer to the Muse of Ordinary Life" from *Four Testimonies*. Copyright © 1997 by Kate Daniels. Used by permission of Kate Daniels.

Carolyn Forché, "The Morning Baking" from *Gathering the Tribes*. Copyright © 1976 by Carolyn Forche. Used by permission of Carolyn Forché. "Expatriate," "Selective Service," "The Colonel," and "For the Stranger" from *The Angel of History* by Carolyn Forché. Copyright © 1994 by Carolyn Forché. Used by permission of HarperCollins Publishers.

John Foy, "Cost" from *No One Leaves the World Unhurt*. Copyright © 2021 by John Foy. Reprinted with the permission of The Permissions Company, LLC on behalf of Autumn House, autumnhouse.org. "Eucalyptus Trees" and "Techne's Clearinghouse" from *Techne's Clearinghouse*. Copyright © 2004 by John Foy. Used by permission of University of Nebraska Press. "Dog" and "Sorrow, Meister Eckhart Said" from *Night Vision*. Copyright © 2016 by John Foy. Used by permission of John Foy.

Dana Gioia, "The Next Poem," "Planting a Sequoia," "Counting the Children," "Interrogations at Noon," "Summer Storm," "Pentecost," "The Angel with the Broken Wing," and "Marriage of Many Years" from *99 Poems: New and Selected*. Copyright © 1986, 1991, 2001, 2012, 2016 by Dana Gioia. Reprinted with the permission of The Permissions Company, LLC on behalf of Graywolf Press, Minneapolis, Minnesota, www.graywolfpress.org.

Marie Howe, "The Star Market," "The Snow Storm," "My Mother's Body," "What We Would Give Up," "Easter," and "Prayer" from *The Kingdom of Ordinary Time*. Copyright © 2008 by Marie Howe. "The Boy" and "What the Living Do" from *What the Living Do*. Copyright © 1997 by Marie Howe. All used by permission of W. W. Norton & Company, Inc.

Brigit Pegeen Kelly, "Petition" and "Song" from *Song*. Copyright © 1995 by Brigit Pegeen Kelly. Reprinted with the permission of The Permissions Company, LLC on behalf of BOA Editions Ltd., boaeditions.org. "The Garden of the Trumpet Tree" and "The Satyr's Heart" from *The Orchard*. Copyright © 2004 by Brigit Pegeen Kelly. Reprinted with the permission of The Permissions Company, LLC on behalf of BOA Editions Ltd., boaeditions.org. "The Visitation" from *To the Place of Trumpets*. Copyright © 1988 by Brigit Pegeen Kelly. Used by permission of Yale University Press.

April Lindner, "Learning to Float" and "Fontanel" from *Skin*. Copyright © 2002 by Texas Tech University Press. Used by permission of Texas Tech University Press. "St. Theresa in Ecstasy," "Our Lady of Perpetual Help," "Carried Away," and "The Trip to Brooklyn Misremembered as a Roller Coaster Ride" from *This Bed Our Bodies Shaped*. Copyright © 2012 by April Lindner. Used by permission of Able Muse Press.

Orlando Ricardo Menes, "Miami, South Kendall, 1969" and "Palma y Jagüey" from *Furia*. Copyright © 2004 by Orlando Ricardo Menes. Used by permission of Orlando Ricardo Menes. "The Maximum Leader Addresses His Island Nation," "Den of the Lioness," and "Juancito's Wake" from *Fetish*. Copyright ©

from *Second Things*. Copyright © 2008 by Daniel Tobin. "An Echo on the Narrows" from *The Net*. Copyright © 2014 by Daniel Tobin. "Aftermath" from *The Narrows*. Copyright © 2005 by Daniel Tobin. All reprinted with the permission of The Permissions Company, LLC on behalf of Four Way Books, fourwaybooks.com. "Homage to Bosch" from *Double Life*. Copyright © 2002 by Daniel Tobin. Used by permission of Louisiana State University Press.

James Matthew Wilson, "See" from *The Hanging God*. Copyright © 2018 by James Matthew Wilson. Used by permission of Angelico Press. "Let Us Tune Our Instruments" from *The River of the Immaculate Conception*. Copyright © 2019 by James Matthew Wilson. Used by permission of Wiseblood Books. "On a Palm" from *Presence Journal*, Spring 2017. Used by permission of James Matthew Wilson. "A Prayer for Livia Grace" from *Some Permanent Things*. Copyright © 2022 by James Matthew Wilson. Used by permission of Wiseblood Books. "March 25, 2020" and "April 15, 2020" from *The Strangeness of the Good*. Copyright © 2020 by James Matthew Wilson. Used by permission of Angelico Press.

Ryan Wilson, "For a Dog," "Face It," and "In the Harvest Season" from *The Stranger World*. Copyright © 2017 by Ryan Wilson. Used by permission of Measure Press. "Disobedience" from *Modern Age*, a publication of the Intercollegiate Studies Institute, Spring 2020. Used by permission of *Modern Age*. "Philoctetes, Long Afterward" from *The Hopkins Review*, Vol. 11. Used by permission of The Hopkins Review. "Heorot" from *The Sewanee Review*, Spring 2019. Used by permission of *The Sewanee Review*.

Franz Wright, "Year One," "P.S.," and "Letter" from *Walking to Martha's Vineyard* by Franz Wright. Copyright © 2003 by Franz Wright. "Transfusion" from *Kindertotenwald: Prose Poems* by Franz Wright, copyright © 2011 by Franz Wright. "Memoir" from *The Beforelife* by Franz Wright, copyright © 2000 by Franz Wright. "Baudelaire" from *Wheeling Motel* by Franz Wright, copyright © 2009 by Franz Wright. "Crumpled-Up Note Blowing Away" from *F: Poems* by Franz Wright, copyright © 2013 by Franz Wright. All used by permission of Alfred A. Knopf, an imprint of the Knopf Doubleday Publishing Group, a division of Penguin Random House LLC. All rights reserved.

David Yezzi, "Crane," "Free Period" and "Minding Rites" from *Birds of the Air*. Copyright © 2013 by David Yezzi. "The Chain" and "Weeds" from *Black Sea*. Copyright © 2018 by David Yezzi. All are reprinted with the permission of The Permissions Company, LLC on behalf of Carnegie Mellon University Press, www.cmu.edu/universitypress. "Tyger, Tyger" from *Literary Matters*, Issue 13.3, Spring/Summer 2021. Used by permission of Literary Matters. "The Good News" and "Mother Carey's Hen" from *Azores*. Copyright © 2008 by Ohio University Press. Used by permission of Ohio University Press.

ABOUT THE EDITORS

Ryan Wilson is editor-in-chief of *Literary Matters* and author of *The Stranger World*, winner of the Donald Justice Poetry Prize, of *How to Think Like a Poet*, winner of the Jacques Maritain Prize, of *Proteus Bound: Selected Translations*, and of *In Ghostlight: Poems*. His work appears widely in periodicals such as *Best American Poetry*, *First Things*, *Five Points*, *Hopkins Review*, *The New Criterion*, *Sewanee Review*, and *Yale Review*. CFO of the Association of Literary Scholars, Critics, and Writers (ALSCW), he teaches at The Catholic University of America and in the MFA program at the University of St. Thomas-Houston.

April Lindner is the author of two poetry collections—*Skin* (winner of the Walt McDonald First Book Prize from Texas Tech University Press) and *This Bed Our Bodies Shaped* (Able Muse Press). She has edited a number of anthologies including *Contemporary American Poetry*, an anthology for Penguin Academics (co-edited with R. S. Gwynn), and *Líneas Conectadas*, for Sarabande Books. She also has written three novels, *Jane*, *Catherine*, and *Love, Lucy*, published by Poppy/Little, Brown Young Reader. A professor in the Department of English, Writing, and Journalism at Saint Joseph's University in Philadelphia, she lives in Stockton, New Jersey.

ABOUT PARACLETE PRESS

PARACLETE PRESS is the publishing arm of the Cape Cod Benedictine community, the Community of Jesus. Presenting a full expression of Christian belief and practice, we reflect the ecumenical charism of the Community and its dedication to sacred music, the fine arts, and the written word.

SCAN
TO
READ
MORE

www.paracletepress.com

IRON
PEN

O that my words were written down!
O that they were inscribed in a book!
O that with an iron pen and with lead
they were engraved on a rock forever!
—JOB 19:23–24

Outcast and utterly alone, Job pours out his anguish to his Maker. From the depths of his pain, he reveals a trust in God's goodness that is stronger than his despair, giving humanity some of the most beautiful and poetic verses of all time. Paraclete's Iron Pen imprint is inspired by this spirit of unvarnished honesty and tenacious hope.

YOU MIGHT BE INTERESTED IN:

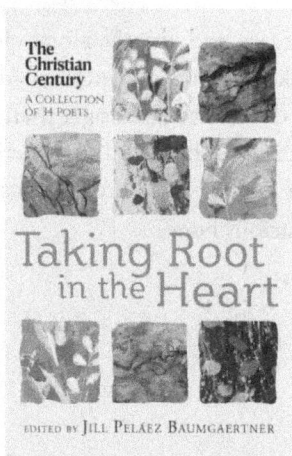

Dear Dante: Poems — Angela Alaimo O'Donnell

Christian Poetry in America Since 1940: An Anthology — Edited by Micah Mattix and Sally Thomas

Reversing Entropy: New Poems — Luci Shaw

Lacunae: New Poems — Scott Cairns

The Christian Century: A Collection of 34 Poets — Taking Root in the Heart — Edited by Jill Peláez Baumgaertner